I joined to
FLY NAVY
What happened next?

James M Milne MBE

Grosvenor House
Publishing Limited

This book is published by
Grosvenor House Publishing Ltd
Link House
140 The Broadway, Tolworth, Surrey, KT6 7HT.
www.grosvenorhousepublishing.co.uk

A CIP record for this book
is available from the British Library

ISBN 978-1-83975-811-9

Front Cover acknowledgements:

Fleet Air Arm Wings are reproduced from author's photograph.

Fly Navy Logo is reproduced with kind permission of the naval charity NavyWings

Fairey Swordfish II LS326 Photo is reproduced with kind permission of Michael West

The background of sky/clouds used a resource from Freepik.com

PREFACE

My sister Susan attempted to get our father, John Milne, to write his life history. We had all heard father talk about what he had been doing during WW2. How he had been in the Home Guard on guard duty with no ammunition; how he had been part of the team that developed the Grand Slam bomb which was used against the submarine pens in Brest, and the warhead on the midget submarines which attacked the German battleship Tirpitz. But they are the only stories that we have, as our father died before committing them to paper.

Realising that we had lost the history of my father's career I determined to find out more about my grandfather who had served in the Royal Navy during WW1. Having assembled the facts, and that is all they were, dates and units served in, I came to realise I knew nothing about what adventures, scrapes, or experiences he had had during his naval career.

What were his thoughts down in the engine room of HMS Glasgow as she disengaged from the one- sided Battle of Coronel and sped away in the darkness to the safety of the Magellan Straits and the Falkland Islands? How did he feel weeks later when at the Battle of the Falklands the Glasgow assisted in sinking those same German ships which had killed so many of his friends?

I decided to record some of my experiences from my 32 year naval career, to give my daughters, son and grandchildren a flavour of what naval life was like during my time in the Royal Navy.

Only when I got into the story writing did I realise how important the time of my naval service had been to the Royal Navy. I had joined in 1960 when the Royal Navy numbered 98,000 with 5 aircraft carriers and 2 commando carriers. Fleet Air Arm flying was very much a matter of 'kick the tyres and light the fires' with few aids to enable the aircrew to complete the task. When I left in 1992 the Royal Navy numbered some 60,000, and the aids provided for aircrew had become much more sophisticated. At this stage I thought, and was advised, that my writings may have a wider appeal. Hence 'I joined to FLY NAVY what happened next?'.

All the events and dits (stories) are written as I remember them, but many years later. I have made an effort not to embellish the dits and to keep them to the point. Most involve humour. My time in the Royal Navy and in particular the Fleet Air Arm was no different to anyone else's experiences. Events such as those I describe were commonplace, not unique.

I hope my reader will read the words and reflect on how life has changed. I just hope that everyone is going to continue having adventures, scrapes and experiences.

JMM   2021

DEDICATION

This book is dedicated to my daughter Fiona (and Ron) and my granddaughter Jessica; my daughter Katy (and Stuart); my son John (and Susan) and grandson Ben and granddaughter Hannah.

AN APOLOGY

Throughout my book there are references to names I have forgotten. Many are names I should have remembered but at the time I had no idea I would be writing this book. Keeping a diary was never my idea of fun. My Fleet Air Arm career began 61 years ago and ended 32 years later. My memory is not what it used to be.

I seek the forbearance of all those whose names I cannot remember. This includes all those Royal Navy and Fleet Air Arm personnel who kept me safe through 32 years; the pilots, the Air Engineers, the Safety Equipment ratings, the Naval Airmen, the Aircrewmen, the Seamen, I could go on. They receive little mention in my book, but without them and their dedication to the task in hand, this book could not have been written.

My 32 year career in the Fleet Air Arm was marked by friendship, a sense of purpose, and a willingness to help from all I met. I am sure my predecessors are finding the Fleet Air Arm has not changed.

ACKNOWLEDGEMENTS

Commander David Hobbs MBE for advice and encouragement

   Dr Steve Bond PhD CEng FRAeS for advice and encouragement

Lieutenant Commander Nigel Hennel AFC for keeping my spirits up

Jon Parkinson of Navywings for advice and encouragement

Jan Eaton for proof reading. (All the mistakes and errors are mine!)

Lesley Lindsay for an early reading followed by bags of encouragement and finally,

My wife, Fiona, who, with great forbearance accepted the hours I spent huddled over a computer without complaint.

INDEX

ILLUSTRATIONS

Chapter 1

THE RECRUITMENT PROCESS

November 1959

'You will not pass any of your A Levels, you should leave school and find a job'. Those were the words ringing in my ears from both my Form Master and my Headmaster, James Cobban, at the end of the 1959 Summer Term at Abingdon School. Due to my emphasis on sport and a lack of application to my studies these words did not come as a surprise to me.

My time in the Air Training Corps had convinced me I wanted to fly, to be a pilot. On summer camp to RAF St Mawgan in 1958 I had the privilege of being in the tail gunners' position in an Avro Lancaster, part of a three aircraft formation on a flight around Cornwall - the final flight of the Lancaster saying goodbye to Cornwall, as they were replaced by the Avro Shackleton.

My grandfather had ended his naval career as a Royal Navy Lieutenant Commander in the Marine Engineering Branch. His Naval Officers sword was something I coveted. My mother suggested that if I wanted to inherit the sword, and fly, – why not join the Fleet Air Arm.? My mother remembered a very handsome young man, Gerald Stride, leaving Downton, near Salisbury, to join the Fleet Air Arm as a pilot during World War 2. It obviously made an impression on her. Some ten years later I was to meet Gerald Stride on a course at the Joint Warfare School at Old Sarum near Salisbury (a stone's throw from where I was born).

It all sounded like a plan to this 17 year old. I completed my application to join the Fleet Air Arm and sent it off. I also

1

applied for other employment such as the Anglo-American Mining Corporation in South Africa saying that I enjoyed the outdoor life. Their reply stated that as I would spend most of my working life down a mine I was probably not suitable! In 1959 there was very little unemployment and school leavers had a whole range of employment opportunities. The war had ended only 14 years before and the country was still recovering from the burden of war debt and trying to build up damaged infrastructure. It is true to say that if you wanted to go into a particular vocation there were opportunities at all levels for school leavers. The Royal Navy wrote back to say I was to attend selection interviews in November 1959 at RAF Hornchurch in Essex.

I travelled from Didcot to Hornchurch, Essex, by train. I do remember it was cold and wet during that whole week. RAF Hornchurch was the Aircrew Assessment and Grading Centre for both the RAF and RN. We did exams, we drove assessment machines which assessed eye/hand coordination, and underwent medical examinations. We stayed in Nissen huts, standard RAF accommodation. There was no heating other than a coal fired brazier in the centre of the hut and the two evenings were spent huddled around this source of heat. It was very similar to the accommodation scenes in wartime movies! After two days those who had been successful in getting through the exams and tests were given a rail warrant to the Admiralty Interview Board (AIB) at HMS Sultan in Gosport and on a Tuesday evening we travelled by train to Portsmouth.

The next two days were spent proving we had the ability to be Fleet Air Arm aircrew. Gym tests where you had to lead a team across a chasm or river using planks, ropes and other aids, and with, of course, someone watching to see you were a good team member. The Chief Petty Officer who had the responsibility for making sure we were in the right place at the right time and who was generally looking after us, was a real gem. His team organised all the gym tests and he briefed each team leader on their task. His brief normally included a small hint as to how best carry out your task. He also gave us all advice about the interviews and how best to conduct ourselves. Without his advice I probably would not have got through the selection process.

The final interviews came. By this time our reduced group knew each other quite well. I had chummed up with a South African, Graham Hoffman. He had left South Africa solely with the intention of joining the Fleet Air Arm. Two members were university graduates who had rather elevated ideas of their own importance. At the final interview the interviewee was told whether or not he had been successful. If successful, the interviewee turned left and came back into the waiting area; if unsuccessful, he turned right, collected his bags and left the establishment. When the two undergraduates failed to appear back in the waiting area we all became slightly nervous. I was lucky. The RN saw something more than just a 17 year old schoolboy and I was selected for aircrew training. I returned home to await a letter telling me when I was to report for training.

When my letter arrived I was disappointed to find out that the aptitude tests had resulted in a better score for Observer than Pilot and I was to report for General Naval Training to HMS THUNDERER in Plymouth on 7 March 1960. On reflection selection for Observer was the right choice. Given what I know now, I did not have the aptitude for Pilot.

I was joining the Supplementary List (SL) on an 8 or 12 year commission. This was a short commission, not a full career commission. Dartmouth graduates were on General List (GL) commissions which gave them a full career. It was possible to transfer from SL to GL at a later stage. By extending my commission I remained on the Supplementary List until retirement.

I left school at the end of the Winter Term 1959 very glad to have left academia behind me, especially Calculus which I never understood and still don't.!

Chapter 2

UNDER TRAINING

March 1960 – June 1961
Royal Naval Engineering College Manadon

The naval part of my life began on Monday 7 March 1960 when I joined HMS THUNDERER, the Royal Navy Engineering College, at Manadon in Plymouth, as a Naval Air Cadet. I arrived at Plymouth Station mid-afternoon in my 'Gieves' outfit. This outfit was provided by Gieves, the naval tailor in Portsmouth, when I was measured for my uniform. Grey trousers, a blazer and a hat. There may have been other bits and pieces that I don't remember. The hat resides on Dartmoor following an exercise from the college.

Transport took us up to the college where we were welcomed by the 'Chief'. I cannot for the life of me remember his name, but he kept us in order and provided excellent support and assistance for those who needed it. There were eighteen of us on 'Hermes Course'.

On arrival at our accommodation we were met by a Lieutenant who outlined the programme for the rest of the day/evening. Recollections are a little hazy as to exactly what took place, but I remember being moved from room to room and finally being interviewed by a panel which consisted of an officer, a doctor, and a psychiatrist. Some of the questions appeared to be rather outlandish. We all thought it was maybe something peculiar to the Royal Navy and no one questioned anything. At an early stage in the evening we had made up our beds in the dormitory. By about

2200 we were all fairly tired and fed up with proceedings so it was a relief to be told to retire to our dormitory and get ready for bed – an officer would be round to inspect us before turning in.

We all duly presented ourselves for inspection by our beds and the officer left, putting off the lights as he went, and shouting 'get turned in'. Which we all did, only to find our beds had been 'apple-pied'.

The entire evening had been organised by the Senior Naval Air Cadet Course They had borrowed uniforms, white coats etc, and had spent the entire evening making us more than a little uncomfortable. They had done the apple-pieing, but now turned up with beer and food for a meet and greet. We all slept well that night.

Then it was down to business. Issue of uniforms, books, journals, meeting the staff, finding the classrooms, etc. The OIC was Lt Cdr Harry Hawksworth, a FAA pilot who had fought in Korea. A fair disciplinarian would be my description. At any one time there would be two courses running doing General Naval Training; learning about marching, saluting, naval customs and so on. The rest of the college consisted of engineering courses lasting from a couple of months to two years. There were engineering workshops and a magnificent Wardroom on a hill overlooking the Manadon area. The engineering courses lived in the Wardroom whilst we lived in much less salubrious surroundings down the hill in Nissan huts. Sharing our accommodation were Iranian Navy Engineering students.

Life was busy. We were not allowed off camp for a period after joining, but eventually we were allowed out on Wednesday evenings and Saturday evenings. There was one exception – Sub Lt Clive Jacobs. Clive had been Royal Naval Rerserve (RNR) and was a former Marks and Spencer manager. He had a small open top sports car, which none of the rest of us could aspire to. As a

Sub Lt he was not as restricted as the rest of us were. Sad to say Clive failed the course because as a Sub Lt he had been expected to lead and be an example to the rest of us, which he failed to do in the eyes of Harry Hawksworth.

We all had to pass the Naval Swimming Test in the baths in Devonport Barracks. This consisted of leaping off the diving board in a boiler suit, two lengths of the swimming pool followed by three minutes of floating. I failed the first test not being a strong swimmer. I was not the only one to fail and it meant coming down to the pool at regular intervals to try again. We all passed eventually.

We fought fires at the Damage Control School at Tamerton Foliot and went sailing in cutters beside the Reserve Fleet opposite Devonport Dockyard. Our boots were 'bulled' to a terrific shine, which various treks across Dartmoor managed to spoil. We

Hermes Course. HMS Thunderer 7 March – 15 June 1960

Ministry of Defence Crown Copyright 1960

attended Divisions (a formal parade) twice a week and put in journal entries once a week. We had to give presentations to our fellow course mates.

We were a mixed bunch. I teamed up with Graham Hoffman, the South African who I met during the recruiting interviews. We got on well and he spent his mid-term leave with me at home in Harwell. Rod Trowsdale, another course member had a wrecked Harley Davidson motorbike in his family barn. Graham was mad about motorbikes, so he transported the bits back to the college and used the college engineering facilities to restore it to working order, including a frame for a sidecar. The entire course (18!) was able to ride on this bike/sidecar combination around the college grounds until the Dean of the college decided it was too dangerous and banned the sidecar. Interesting whilst it lasted.

I was now being paid a regular wage. £4 a week. Each fortnight we lined up at the pay parade with our pay books. I bought a motorbike, a Bantam Beezer for £8. I took it by train to Harwell and back again, and then sold it for £8!

At the end of our course we saluted the college with a drive past the Wardroom; salute was taken by Clive in his sports car, flanked by myself and Graham on motorbikes. Graham qualified as a Gannet pilot and was killed in a night time mid-air collision, south of The Lizard, in the mid-60s.

The college Wardroom was a modern building where we took all our meals and attended mess dinners. There were probably around 250 members of the Wardroom including the college instructional staff. Most were on courses and there was a lot of course rivalry. There were also a lot of mess games. One example of the rivalry and ferocity of the games followed a good mess dinner and lots of wine! It was time to play a game which involved placing a number of armchairs in line, with the aim of the game being that a person ran at the chairs from behind, did a somersault and landed up sitting in the furthest armchair. As the feat was achieved another armchair would be added to the line. We had a lot of rivalry with the Long Engineering Course and took them on. All was going well until one of our team, Dave Cant, misjudged his flight and instead of doing the somersault his mouth collided with the back of a strongly built armchair. There was blood everywhere, teeth everywhere and he needed medical attention. We tried to get Dave out of the Mess, but the Long Course wanted him to stay! The result was a total melee of bodies. In the melee one of our team, Bob Christie, had his arm broken. Bob was a bit of a character and being older than most of us had a high opinion of himself. He had crossed the Long Course before. One of our course, John Williams, had a Morris 8, basically a matchbox. He fetched his Morris 8 to transport the wounded to the sickbay. John pulled up outside the Wardroom where the melee was still going on and we dragged Dave and Bob from it and somehow got them into the car. The Long

Royal Naval Engineering College MANADON. 1st XV 1960

Ministry of Defence Crown Copyright 1960

HMS Thunderer Wardroom 1960

Ministry of Defence Crown Copyright 1960

Course decided this was not going to happen, raised the sides of the bonnet and tried to set fire to the engine. Eventually the car broke free and headed off the long way round to the sickbay which was by our accommodation. We, as a course, sped down to the accommodation/sickbay the short way, pursued by the Long Course. There was a bit of a hullabaloo going on which alerted the Iranian cadets who shared our accommodation (they did not attend mess dinners for religious reasons). Out came the Iranians, rolling up their sleeves, to assist us in repelling the Long Course! After a bit of a stand-off the Long Course retreated back to the Wardroom, Dave and Bob were treated in the sickbay. All agreed it had been an enjoyable evening.

One of the instructors at the Engineering College was Lieutenant John Stocker. He had married Jacqueline the daughter of a landlady my father had lived with when he worked in Portsmouth. John lived just outside a side gate to the establishment, close to our accommodation. As a staff member he had a key to this gate. I arranged for Wendy, my girlfriend from Abingdon, to stay with the Stocker's for a week and with his key I was able to slip out and see her every night in the Stocker's married quarter. She was a keen horsewoman and I remember we went for a horse ride at Yelverton just outside Plymouth on the edge of Dartmoor. Never again.

On the days we were allowed out one of our favourite haunts was the GX, or the Plymouth Sailing Club. Somehow it had attracted the name Groin Exchange, hence GX. It was hardly a den of vice. It had a bar, some music and it was cheap. I do remember meeting Clive Sullivan there. He was a Great Britain Rugby League and Hull Kingston Rovers player. There is now a street in Hull called Clive Sullivan Way in his honour.

Parade work took up a lot of our time and from time to time the Senior course had to provide a guard for the ceremony of 'Colours' in front of the Wardroom. Rifles were used with bayonets fixed. An incident sticks in my mind when Eric Newbiggin, given the order 'eyes front' after 'dressing' brought his hand down on the top of the bayonet belonging to the cadet on his right. Straight through the middle of the hand, blood everywhere, and for a minute or two he remained to attention. Eric went on to qualify as a Sea Vixen pilot.

Sport was a big thing at Manadon and two of us, Colin McLennan and me, were selected for the college 1st XV which played in the Devon and Cornwall Rugby League. It was rough, tough rugby and thoroughly enjoyable.

Coming to the end of our time at Manadon as a course we needed to leave our mark. One of the earlier courses had climbed the nearby Police radio mast and left a large flag at the top. We needed to do something. The plan was to steal all the cutlery from Dartmouth Naval College overnight. None of us had ever been to Dartmouth so Bob Christy borrowed a uniform and visited Dartmouth on a reconnaissance. Following his visit and report back, three members were chosen for the raid, me, Bob Christy and John Williams, as he had the Morris 8. We arrived at the College at about 0100. We then spent two hours going around the college dining rooms looking for the cutlery. We never found any! Why? Because it was in drawers in the oak panelling lining the dining halls. So much for the reconnaissance. We left empty handed. Probably just as well as in truth the Morris 8 would have collapsed under the weight of cutlery.

On 15 June 1960, fifteen of us passed out from Manadon, having lost Jacobs, Hudson and Messiter. Only two were now bound for Observer training, Dick Gravestock and me.

HMS ARIEL - Seafield Park

Next stop HMS ARIEL, or Seafield Park, at Lee on Solent, the Safety Equipment and Survival Training School. We arrived there on 17 June 1960. Two more people destined for Observer training joined us, David Dobson, a General List Lieutenant and Neville

Survival Course HMS Ariel June 1960

Ministry of Defence Crown Copyright 1960

The author preparing to survive! HMS Ariel 1960

Ministry of Defence Crown Copyright 1960

Truter. Over the next four weeks we were issued with our flying safety equipment; helmets; a Talbe set (emergency radio); Mae West, goonsuits etc.

A 'goonsuit was a two piece waterproof suit designed to keep aircrew dry in the event of landing in the water. Rubber cuffs and neckpiece made the top half waterproof and by rolling up the rubber rings at the bottom of the top half and at the top of the trousers it was possible to be watertight. Taking the goonsuit off could be tricky if it was a slightly smaller size than was needed. I have seen normally level headed aircrew get to panic stations attempting to take the top of their goonsuit off. Happily, technology moved on and later goonsuits were one piece with a waterproof zip and rubber neckpiece and much more comfortable. We were shot up a ramp on an ejection seat!

Three things are memorable from this time. Firstly a doctor at the nearby Naval Medical Centre at Alverstoke, had come up with an idea that he could predict our medical category by putting us individually into a pressure tank, simulate high altitude by evacuating the oxygen, and feed us a gas mixture to breath. It was not a pleasant experience being in this small tank with the hatch being screwed down and a little window to look out through. We all went through the tank and I presume the results were compared with the medical categories that we were awarded.

Secondly we all went through the diving tank at HMS DOLPHIN in Gosport. We all had to do two runs from the 30ft depth which meant being put into a blister off the tank at 30ft. The water would be let in to equalise the pressure, you would then duck out through a hatch into the tank and would rise to the surface remembering to blow out as you ascended. It was here I found I am 'negatively buoyant' and had to wear a special cap for identification. The two runs were uneventful. Once we all assembled at the top of the tank with the instructors Dave Cant asked if he could do the 60ft ascent. The instructor instead of saying 'who would like to do the 60ft', said, ' is there anyone who would not like to do the 60ft'?. Of course no one wanted to say 'no'. We all found ourselves doing the 60ft ascent which seemed like forever. Luckily it is not permitted to do the 100ft ascent on the same day as you have done the 60ft otherwise we would have been down there for sure.

The final memory is the Survival Course itself. It took place over a week, all in the New Forest. Effectively we were escaping aircrew in hostile territory making for an RV on the coast. Most courses were met by a minesweeper and taken off the beach back to Gosport. We were to return by coach as no ship was available! I do remember day one. It started at the bridge over the River Avon at Ringwood. We were divided into 4/5 man teams and each team member had a one man dinghy. We had to make an RV down the Avon. Off we went, without too much paddling as the current was taking us along. Round a bend and there at the side of the Avon was a cow stuck fast in the mud and obviously in trouble. We all paddled to the bank and set about getting the cow up onto the bank some six feet above the river. It was a large cow and you can imagine what we looked like after probably an hour's exertion. On we went. We spent the next few days crisscrossing the New Forest, eating unimaginable things and generally wondering what all this was achieving. Come the last night the Officer In Charge of Seafield Park, an old and gnarled Lt Cdr (Joe), appeared with, beer, real food and half a dozen young ladies! This was survival with a difference. The young ladies were working in a local hostelry which Joe frequented and had volunteered to come and cheer us up! It was all above board, we all turned in early ready to catch our coach the next morning. On Saturday 16 July 1960 we left Seafield Park for a flight to Malta to start Observer training in earnest.

HMS FALCON

Following the BEA Viscount flight to Malta I started No 49 Observer training course at HMS FALCON (Royal Navy Air Station Hal Far) on 18 July 1960. Our Course Officer was

Lt Arthur White, ex Sea Venom Observer. David Dobson, Neville Truter, Dick Gravestock, and I were joined by Chris Wilson (a failed Pilot Course GL Lt) and Stuart Brickell (whose history I forget).

Looking at my logbook for August 1960 it would appear we started early as the majority of take offs were at 0700 in our Sea Princes. We learnt to operate the radar and did navigation exercises. We also visited the pubs in Kalafrana and drank Cisk and Hopleaf, Maltese synthetic beers (not nice). Into September and there were night navigation exercises and on 20 September Exercise Scatter. Exercise Scatter involved all military aircraft in Malta simulating a possible attack on Maltese airfields and scattering to the four winds. My Sea Prince ended up at RAF Idris in Libya, where we had lunch and then headed back to Hal Far. The Station Heron collected four Wrens and headed for Athens, not to be seen again for a number of days! Into October with more Navigation exercises, photographic sorties, radar check flights and a familiarisation in a Meteor from the Target Towing Squadron. As the Meteor cockpit canopy was being brought down I managed to leave my arm outside resulting in the canopy crushing my aircrew watch. Luckily the watch was there otherwise I would have broken my wrist.

Part of our training included an escape and evasion exercise. All of the courses in the Observer school were involved and the Hunter Force was the resident Royal Marine Commando from St Georges Barracks. All trainee Observers were divided into three man teams. We were dropped off in the north of the island with a grid reference to aim for. We had been briefed on our background which was that we were the crew of a naval aircraft sent to bomb a certain target. Dropped just before nightfall we three, myself, Neville Truter and Fred Mills set off cross country. Malta is not flat and farmers arranged their fields in terraces backed by stone walls which can be quite high. Overnight we made what we thought was good progress considering there was no moon. We confidently tackled the stone walls making as little noise as possible. All was going well until we arrived at a stone wall where it was difficult to see how far down the ground was.

Neville thought he could see the ground lowered himself down a couple of feet and let go. There was a splash and a curse. Neville had dropped into a Maltese compost/sewer pool about four feet deep. Luckily his mouth had been closed on landing! Fred and I moved a few feet to the side and completed a dry landing. To say Neville stank would be an understatement, but we moved on with Neville bringing up the rear. Up to this point we had seen no sign of the Royal Marines. It was just beginning to get light. We dropped down a stone wall into a field of large cabbages and had been walking down the side of the field when there was a clink like a metal cup. The three of us sank down between the rows of rather large cabbages which covered us completely. Looking down the row I saw a figure walking across the bottom of the field and indicated to Fred who was about two feet in front of me to keep down. Fred immediately got to his feet, at which point the line of Royal Marines who were lying in wait charged across the field and we offered little resistance. It was only afterwards we found out that everyone was to be captured, the only routes that could be used were known to the Royal Marines, they just laid their ambushes in the right place. We were blindfolded and put in a 3 tonner (with all the rest who had been captured!) and taken to St Georges Barracks. We were kept blindfolded, no talking, standing against a wall, hands tied behind our backs. Every now and then someone would be taken away and one would come back. This was not part of the exercise that we knew anything about! Then it was my turn. Into a room, blindfold removed and there were three Royal Marine interrogators sitting in front of me at a desk and they all looked like mean characters. The questioning began and in true 'film' style I refused to answer their questions and realised why we had been given a 'story' before setting out. I became aware of someone standing behind me. At this point I knew I was amongst friends and that they would not deliberately harm me, but at the same time you wonder how far they would go. I soon found out. Dragged out of my seat, into another room, flat on my back on the floor, a damp cloth put on my face and water poured onto the cloth. All sorts of thoughts go through your head. Is this real? Will I die? Who knows I am here? How long it lasted I don't know, but thankfully I didn't drown. Cloth removed, blindfold back on, dragged to my feet, into another room. Stand at the wall. Then suddenly moved through a door, blindfold removed, you are free, into 3 tonner, back to Hal Far. Everyone had been captured, everyone went through the same routine, everyone was glad that was all over. My reaction was that I vowed never to be caught again on an escape and evasion exercise especially if Royal Marines are involved.

Into November with a bit of cold creeping in and time for our passing out parade on 17 November. I scraped through with 3rd Class passes in the Air and on the Ground. I was destined for anti-submarine helicopters and not Sea Vixens or Gannets. Although disappointed at the time it was the best path for me, as I came to realise later. My final two flights, on 15 November were on search and rescue missions searching for a target towing Meteor crew who had been cooperating with HMS GIRDLE NESS on Sea Slug missile trials and had disappeared off the radar. Nothing was ever found.

The things I remember from Malta are very few probably because I was concentrating on passing the course. There were no wild parties and, going sailing in the station yacht was not something I enjoyed due to sea sickness. I visited most of the historic sites in Malta which I did enjoy. But, the mess dinner in November to mark the Battle of Taranto was memorable. The Battle of Taranto took place on the night of 11/12 November 1940. The Royal Navy launched the first all aircraft ship-to-ship naval attack in history employing 21 Swordfish biplane torpedo bombers from HMS ILLUSTRIOUS in an attack on Italian Navy ships in Taranto Harbour. The Italian Navy had one battleship disabled, one heavy cruiser damaged and two destroyers damaged. The Fleet Air Arm lost two aircraft with one crew being taken prisoner and one crew being killed. The Captain of Hal Far, AWF (Alfie) Sutton, had been part of the raid on Taranto, so his speech was dedicated to the raid and his part in it with his pilot 'Tiffy' Torrens-Spence, for which they were both awarded the DSC. Captain Sutton retired in 1965 and died in November 2008. There were Swordfish suspended from wires in the ceiling going backwards and forwards. I was sitting next to a Wrens Officer. The officer sitting on my left and I decided to enliven proceedings with some cigar tube missiles. Easy to make – place a number of match heads in a cigar tube, jam a second cigar tube in the top, heat the bottom of the tube with the match heads in, the result is an explosion which sends the second cigar tube across the Wardroom. If you jam the second cigar tube down too hard, as we did, the explosion melts the area around the match-heads and they go backwards. Inevitably the fireball of match heads landed on the Wrens Officers dress and the dress caught fire. Wrens Officer was last seen heading for the heads at a rate of knots. We ascertained the next day that she was alright; but she did not return to the mess dinner.

The nearest I came to romance was during a night navigation exercise when a young Wren came along as a familiarisation. It is 25 October 1960 and I was coming to the end of my course. The morning had been spent in a 750 Squadron Sea Prince T Mk 1 on a map reading exercise in the Low Fly Area in Sicily and I was being briefed on the final night sortie of the course – Night Navex No 4.

Unusually there was a young Wren kitted out in flying clothing attending the briefing. Once the briefing was over my Course Officer, Lt Arthur White, introduced my pilot, Lt Cdr Proyer, and me to the youngster and told me she would be sitting in on my sortie as part of her introduction to operations at Hal Far. I had not been the best Observer student and needed to get good marks from this sortie. That is where my mind was focussed.

The take off and initial parts of the sortie went smoothly enough and everything including my brain was working normally. The young Wren sitting alongside of me had not said anything and I was too busy to talk to her. My nav chart was unusually neat and tidy, not too many extra lines or crossings out.

Hunting Percival TMk 1 Sea Prince – the flying classroom

Reproduced by kind permission of Chris England

Suddenly, young Wren picked up my navigational compasses and appeared to say something to me, difficult to tell behind the oxygen mask. I heard nothing and indicated to her to switch her microphone on – but that did not help. By this time I had retrieved my compasses from her grasp - but in return she had taken my nav computer. We were approaching a turning point and I could have done without the distractions of a thieving Wren. By now she was twiddling away on the settings on the nav computer and indicating that she would like to know how it worked.

I remember the next few moments well. Should I make use of the compasses by stabbing her hand or would a quick stab in the leg get the message through? Luckily for her I remembered this was a short leg and needed a radar fix before the next turning point. I turned away and squinted down into the radar screen. Back to my chart and – where was my pencil? You would have thought she knew what a pencil was! And so we continued through the two hour sortie. Her headset and microphone were U/S (unserviceable), so in order to keep her hands off my equipment I wrote notes on my chart informing her what was happening.

I failed Night Navex 4 because I had an untidy chart, not because I was in the wrong place at the wrong time or uncertain of my position!

I passed my Observer Training more by luck than ability and certainly not helped by one young Wren whom I never met again.

My lasting memories of Sea Prince flying in Malta are Lt Chris Blanchett flying up a sea inlet with the wingtips grazing the tops of the cliffs whilst the fuselage was still beneath the tops and wondering if he was going to pull up in time, and the sortie to RAF Idris in Libya on Exercise Scatter where the aim appeared to be to get as much Brandy in the aircraft as possible for the return trip.

HMS OSPREY

Leaving Malta in late November I joined HMS Vernon in Portsmouth for a Torpedo and Anti-Submarine Course from 21 November to 2 December 1960. And finally arrived at HMS Osprey, Portland, on 5 December 1960 for No 17 Anti-Submarine Operational Flying Training Course. It must have been ground school up until Christmas as I did not start flying until January 1961.

We now met up with pilots who were under training so everyone was learning. Our workhorse was the Whirlwind HAS Mk 7 not known as the most reliable helicopter. We plunged into the mysteries of navigating a helicopter, dipping sonar, and winching. Our instructors were Dick Van de Plank, Dereck Beesley, and David Husband. Other trainee Observers on the course were David Dobson, Neville Truter, and Fred Mills. On 16 January I learnt about the unreliability of the Mk 7 when out on an anti-submarine exercise our consort Mk 7 ditched.

As part of our training we spent a day at sea in a submarine. In my case it was HM S/M THULE. THULE had been launched in October 1942 and spent most of WW2 in the Far East. In November 1960 she had been rammed by RFA Black Ranger off Portland with damage to her periscope and conning tower. Two things remain in my memory. I sat in the Wardroom whilst we dived off Portland and as we sank into the depths a drip of water started leaking through the deckhead which required a bucket to catch the drips. On enquiring as to the reason for this drip I was informed it was quite normal and as THULE was being taken out of service to be scrapped it was not regarded as a problem! Then I was taken to get a briefing on the 'heads' (toilet). In order for the flushing mechanism to work correctly there was a sequence of valves to be opened and closed in the correct order. At the bottom of the toilet bowl was a metal flap which was held in place by a large bolt. Whilst going through the correct sequence of valves the flap would open and the contents get sucked away. If the correct sequence was not followed two events took place. Firstly the outside pressure would build up such that the bolt would be explosively discharged from the flap and secondly the contents of the bowl would be discharged upwards. The consequences could be death if the bolt caught you on its way upwards or as it bounced around the compartment, and of course you would be covered in the bowl contents. In the deckhead were a number of large dents as proof. It was an interesting day which convinced me never to be a submariner. THULE was scrapped in September 1962.

I progressed through the course which I really enjoyed. On 18 March 1961 my Record of Service states 'Has successfully completed No 17 A/S Helicopter OFS Course. With more experience should make an average Squadron Observer'. I was presented with my Observer Wings on 18 March 1961 by Rear Admiral Frank Hopkins, the Flag Officer Flying Training. I was a happy bunny.

As I was not immediately being sent to a squadron I remained with 737 Squadron, the training squadron, until 22 June. Flying was varied, acting as a Sonar Operator for other courses coming through and flying on ships inspections.

I was destined for 825 Squadron embarked in HMS VICTORIOUS and currently operating somewhere East of Suez. I thought my training was over. How wrong can you be!

Chapter 3

HMS VICTORIOUS

825 Squadron/Whirlwind HAS Mk 7 – June 1961 to April 1962

M y first front line squadron was 825 Squadron equipped with Whirlwind Mk7 helicopters and based on HMS Victorious.

As Victorious was in the Persian Gulf reinforcing the naval presence as Iraq threatened Kuwait my journey to join her was quite exciting to a young Midshipman. In the first week of July I took a trooping flight from RAF Lyneham to RAF Muharraq in Bahrain, a transit through HMS JUFAIR, the shore base in Bahrain, and onto Mina Sulman jetty to HMS CHICHESTER, an anti-submarine frigate. Then an overnight passage to the northern Persian Gulf. No room onboard and I slept on a camp-bed on the bridge wing for the passage north.

Up a scrambling net and I had arrived. Victorious was in the middle of what was then to be the longest sea-going deployment by an aircraft carrier to date. That record has since been well beaten.

It was July, it was hot and humid and Victorious was not air-conditioned. Everyone had 'prickly heat', basically a rash from sweating all the time! There was a shortage of water as the evaporators were old and kept on failing and showers were limited to literally stepping in and stepping out. Sleeping was a problem and even more so for the officer who was sleeping on the Quarterdeck on top of a grating and who rolled over the side as the ship turned. He was recovered, no worse for wear.

As the new boy in a war zone I was made almost a permanent Duty Officer. What is a Squadron Duty Officer (SDO) ? In effect the SDO is responsible for the squadron routine for the next 24 hours. You would take over the duty following a handover at 0800. If it is a flying day at sea you are responsible for running the flying programme which means ensuring crews get briefed on time, ensuring that changes to the Flying Programme (Flypro) are promulgated, liaising with the squadron engineers to ensure that aircraft are serviceable; organising pilots for engine runs; liaising with Flyco (Flying Control Position) and the Flight Deck Officers (FDOs) to ensure aircraft are ready to be moved to meet the Flight Deck programme. In between times you may have to deal with a squadron disciplinary matter and generally prepare to be responsible for everything that is thrown at you. Being Duty Officer on a strike carrier in a long major NATO exercise or operational situation is worth a book on its own! I learnt quickly. When alongside or disembarked it does not get any easier. Still looking after the Flypro but now the squadron Commanding Officer wants you, for example, to look after some visitors, in addition to any other little task the Senior Pilot/Senior Observer or Air Engineering Officer dreams up. In between times to make sure I was occupied I found myself as Third Officer of the Watch on the bridge.

Relieved by HMS CENTAUR at the end of July it was time to leave the Gulf. Victorious made her way to Mombasa for rest/relaxation/maintenance, arriving on 8 August.

The question of new boy came up again and as custom had it the squadron provided the For'ard Officer of the Watch. Guess who was 'lumbered' with the task for the first 24 hours in port! Victorious anchored in Kilindini Harbour and had to run boats to and from the shore. It would be an interesting 24 hours.

Victorious had just completed a long hot deployment and it was the first day of shore leave and I had the job of For'ard

Officer of the Watch from 1600 to 2000, then from 0001 until 0400. The boat routine had to run like clockwork to get 1000 matelots (sailors) ashore and also to get them back. I was lucky the Quartermaster and the Bosun's Mate were experienced hands and kept me right. The Master at Arms (Naval Police) kept an eye on goings on and from 1600 to 2000 the boat routine ran to time and it appeared the entire Ships Company had decided to 'go for a stroll' in the town of Mombasa.

Returning to the For'ard Boat Deck at midnight was a bit different. From the boatloads coming back from shore it was obvious that during their stroll in Mombasa many had been enticed into various drinking halls and pubs. To be drunk onboard is a punishable offence, however to get around this rule if the Officer of the Watch was happy that the Leading Hand of the Mess or other suitable person was prepared to look after the 'happy drunk' then they could proceed to their Mess Deck. Unfortunately we had dozens of happy drunks appearing on a regular basis from the ships boats, most of them out of their tiny minds. So we laid them out along the deck, firstly to stop them falling over the side, secondly to stop them milling around and possibly lose them in the throng, and thirdly so that we could call Leading Hands of the Mess down and be able to point out their messmate. I remember we had 84 bodies laid out at one point. Ashore the Naval Shore Patrol was organising matelots getting into the ships boats and persuading those who thought they could swim back not to do so. That night nobody tried to swim back. A few nights later someone did attempt to swim and was almost certainly taken by the sharks which we had been warned were always patrolling the harbour.

The remainder of my time in my first Front Line squadron was taken up with listening and learning, interspersed with various runs ashore in Singapore and Hong Kong. The squadron disembarked to RNAS Sembawang from 9 September to 4 October 1961. Many runs ashore were momentous and I will draw a veil across most of them.

On VICTORIOUS the planeguard was provided by 824 Squadron, but on later carriers there were two dedicated Whirlwind Mk 9's as a Search & Rescue (SAR) Unit. VICTORIOUS also had an old Gannet AS4 used as the Carrier on Delivery (COD) aircraft for fetching mail, VIP visitors, stores etc. On later carriers COD services were provided by the Search and Rescue Whirlwind 9s. The planeguard was there to provide rescue services in the event that an aircraft had a problem on launch or during recovery. About 150 yds off the port quarter for recovery; 100 yds away and at right angles to the catapult launcher for launches. Divers only became part of the planeguard equipment with the dedicated SAR Flights.

I have already mentioned that I joined the Fleet Air Arm partly due to a reminiscence by my mother about a certain Gerald Stride leaving Downton to join the Fleet Air Arm. In researching this book I have discovered that in the accompanying picture the aircraft joining the 825 Squadron Whirlwinds in formation on VICTORIOUS, somewhere in the Mediterranean, is the RNAS Hal Far Search and Rescue Sikorsky S-55 Whirlwind piloted by none other than Gerald Stride! Small world.

Training for planeguard involved wet winching with single and double lifts involving all carrier-borne aircrew. In the warm Far East waters there were plenty of volunteers; in home waters it was a bit more difficult. The Sproule net, basically a clam shaped net with a metal frame and a drogue, which could be dragged through the water to recover a body (dead or alive), was also used. Many hours were spent practising recovering oil drums with the Sproule Net. We never used 'live bodies' during Sproule Net training, the potential for injury was too great. The Sproule Net had been invented by John Sproule, Commanding Officer of 700(H) Squadron the Whirlwind HAS Mk 7 Intensive Flying Trials Unit in 1957.

All carriers have a 'Goofers'. This is an area normally in the 'island' on the upper works where those off watch could come up and take the air and watch flying operations. On occasion the

825 Squadron Whirlwind HAS Mk 7 joined by the Search and Rescue Whirlwind HAS Mk 22 from RNAS Hal Far, in formation on HMS Victorious. 1961

Ministry of Defence Crown Copyright 1961

carrier would stream a 'Splash Target' astern. The Splash Target was a 'sledge' with a scoop which would produce a fountain of water thereby giving the fixed wing aircraft a target. It would be attacked by rockets and practice bombs from Scimitars, Sea Vixens and later on by Buccaneers. By taking a bearing from the carrier and from the planeguard helicopter which would be stationed at right angles to the ships course abeam the Splash Target it was possible to get a reasonable idea of the accuracy of the attacks. The Goofers were normally packed for Splash Target work.

For those interested in sport and keeping fit there were a number of options on a carrier. There were plenty of spaces where an impromptu gym could be set up. When the flight deck was not being used there was an ideal running track available or space just for strolling and taking the air. For those into team sport there was deck hockey and volleyball. Deck hockey was played with what can best be described as walking sticks and a 'puck' made

825 Squadron Whirlwind HAS Mk 7 deck move on HMS Victorious. 1961

All eight 825 Squadron Whirlwind HAS Mk 7 disembarking from HMS Victorious to RNAS Sembawang. 1961

Ministry of Defence Crown Copyright 1961

825 Squadron Whirlwind HAS Mk 7 on patrol in South China Sea accompanied by water - spout. 1961

HMS Victorious, 'The Gray Lady' turning at speed. 1961

Ministry of Defence Crown Copyright 1961

825 Squadron 1961

Ministry of Defence Crown Copyright 1961

of a small coiled rope covered in black duct tape. For impromptu games there were no rules and injuries could appear all over one's body. For inter-departmental games at least the number of players on each side would be agreed! Volleyball was played on the aircraft lifts and time was set aside within the working day when the lifts would be not be working. Volleyball teams were six and a lot of interdepartmental, league and knockout competitions were played. With the lift down railings were put up on the flight deck and for knockout competitions there were lots of supporters. I was a keen volleyball player and probably one of my more frightening experiences must rank as a competition final between 848 Squadron volleyball team and that of the embarked Commando. The entire Commando turned out as spectators some 20 feet above the playing surface. Royal Marines (RMs) tend to be quite passionate about their sport and of course winning. The noise, the abuse and the hate that rained down upon us was something to be experienced only once in one's career. I cannot remember who won but I suspect the RMs may have just edged it!

The Whirlwind HAS 7 had a piston engine, the Alvis Leonides Major. For maintenance purposes it had a hand crank to turn the engine over. The squadron Chief Aircraft Artificer, Chief Webb, had a theory that it should be possible to start the engine using this hand crank much as car engines used to be started. On a very hot day he set off to prove his theory and 'hey presto' after an age of cranking the engine it finally spluttered into life. Chief Webb is probably the only man alive who has achieved this feat.

Whirlwind HAS 7s had a record of ditching quite frequently. In 825 Squadron we had done rather well and the rumour was that if we finished our time on Victorious without a ditching Westland Helicopters Ltd would stand the squadron to a slap up dinner. We almost made it. On a grey day, 13 February, in the English Channel I was Squadron Duty Officer and watching one of our aircraft off the port quarter of VICTORIOUS when the tail rotor disintegrated. It was on a test flight with the Senior Pilot and Senior Observer up front and two aircraft maintainers in the back. The Senior Pilot was a large burly gentleman and as the aircraft settled in the water and rolled to port he released his harness and began to exit the cockpit. The Senior Observer in the left hand seat was small and wiry and was not too pleased with what he thought was a leisurely exit by the Senior Pilot, especially as he was now under the water following the roll to port. He took his navigational dividers from their stowage on his arm and thrust them with some force into the backside of the exiting Senior Pilot. Standing on the deck I was unaware of this mini-drama and was just relieved to see four heads bobbing around once the aircraft had disappeared from view.

I have mentioned already the role of the Squadron Duty Officer. Alongside in Portsmouth I had the duty and Lt Cdr Johnny Ashton, the squadron Commanding Officer asked me to host a former Fleet Air Arm pilot and show him around the ship. The name of the gentleman in question has long passed from my memory, but his story has not. He was serving in 825 Squadron (Swordfish) in May 1941 when the squadron was ordered to embark in VICTORIOUS in the Clyde at short notice. He then took part in the hunt for the Bismarck which led to an attack by 9 Swordfish (825 Squadron) and 2 Fulmar (809 Squadron) on 21 May 1941. The attack was not successful in disabling the Bismarck but all Swordfish returned to VICTORIOUS, the two Fulmar ran out of fuel and had to ditch. During my guided tour of VICTORIOUS the gentleman asked if we could see the compartment where he had slung his hammock which was the Captain's day cabin beneath the Quarterdeck. There were tears in his eyes when we entered the cabin and the hooks where he had slung his hammock were still in place!

On 31 March 1962, Lieutenant Paul Barton, and myself had the honour of acting as planeguard for the last catapult launch from VICTORIOUS before going into refit, – a piano. There was a tradition that the Wardroom piano was despatched to a watery grave at the end of a commission. We then completed the last land-on of the commission. Job done.

One of the COs last tasks when an officer left a squadron was to deliver the officer's 'flimsy'. A flimsy was a very short summing up of the officer's performance during his time in the squadron, normally drafted by the CO and signed by the Captain of the ship. My first, dated 2 April 1962, read,

'during which time he has conducted himself to my entire satisfaction. A pleasant young officer who has tried hard and shows promise'

The important feature here is 'my entire satisfaction'. The CO was quite at liberty to omit the 'entire', or even worse to make it read 'conducted himself to his own satisfaction'.

The flimsy presumably acquired the nickname as the officer's copy was on paper almost as thin as rice paper and measured 3 ½ ins by 6 ½ ins. By 1970 it was on normal paper and had been given a form number, the S450, but was still known as the flimsy.

VICTORIOUS was going into refit and 825 Squadron was disbanded.

Chapter 4

HMS ANZIO (LANDING SHIP TANK)

PERSIAN GULF. May – December 1962

When 825 Squadron disbanded there were no appointments in other squadrons for Observers and we were all sent to sea appointments. I was selected for a minesweeper based in Malta. Arthur Stevens, a recently married Observer was selected for an LST in the Persian Gulf. On finding that he was unable to get a Married Quarter in Bahrain, but could in Malta, he asked if I would swop appointments. Being unmarried without a care in the world, I agreed. My second RAF trooping flight to Bahrain.

HMS ANZIO was a Landing Ship Tank, part of the Amphibious Warfare Squadron based in Bahrain. The Squadron consisted of 2 LSTs Anzio and Messina, plus three smaller Mk 8 Landing Craft Tank,HMS Bastion, HMS Redoubt and HMS Rampart. Not all were present in the Persian Gulf some being absent on refit or other duties. Anzio weighed in at 2200 tons which, with eight 51 ton Centurion tanks and a Beach Armoured Recovery Vehicle (BARV), ammunition etc, went up to over 5000 tons. Armed with 4 x 40mm Bofors, Anzio steamed along at an average of 12 knots. In addition, 6 x Mk 2 Landing Craft Vehicle & Personnel (LCVPs), a Landing Craft Navigation (LCN) used for surveying landing sites and reconnaissance, plus Landing Craft Royal Marines and Officer Commanding Royal Marines (OCRM) were embarked. We also had a doctor and sick bay. Our immediate boss in the Gulf was the Senior Naval Officer Persian Gulf or SNOPG as he was known, based in HMS JUFAIR the Bahrain shore base.

When I joined, our resident tank squadron came from 17th/21st Lancers which in 1993 became the Queens Royal Lancers.

As a junior officer in ANZIO one of the tasks I picked up was Sports Officer. Not too arduous a duty as there were lots of the ships company and the Royal Marine contingent interested in sport and therefore willing to help. I also became the Wines and Spirits Officer responsible for the Wardroom Bar. Ensuring that the Captain had a plentiful supply of Irish Mist Whisky was my most important task.

My finest sporting hour was when as a motley crew, not all dressed in the same jerseys or shorts, we took on the rugby 15 from RAF Muharraq (dressed in an immaculate black strip) on a sand pitch at RAF Muharraq and beat them convincingly. Our 6ft 7in OCRM, Chris had a lot to do with our victory.

My other sports memory is not quite so impressive. ANZIO had anchored off Das Island for a couple of days and it was arranged with the oil company on Das that we would play them at cricket on Day 2. Das Island was a men only island producing oil in the southern Persian Gulf. It was unique in that personnel serving on Das had to take leave every three months or so. The oil company would fly the employee back home or even pay for the family to meet half-way in a holiday destination. The ship's cricket captain was a Leading Seaman whose name is lost in the mists of time. He contacted me during the morning and asked if the team should go ashore 'in rig' (uniform), or in sports gear.

As we are talking about temperatures of 30 deg Celcius plus ashore I judged it reasonable they should go ashore in sports gear. Leading Seaman beetled off and informed the team. Just before lunch I went up to the Iron Deck to see the team off ashore only to find they were all 'in rig'. What's all this about ? I enquired? Leading Seaman replied that the 1st Lieutenant, (a very 'anchor-faced' Lt Cdr), had said they should go 'in rig' not sports gear.

'Ah', I said, 'I don't care what the 1st Lt said, I said sports gear and that is what you will go ashore in'. I looked at all the ashen faces in front of me which appeared to be looking behind me. Turning round I see the 1st Lt standing behind me. The sports team went ashore in rig! I received one month's stoppage of leave, which added to one month I had been awarded for refusing to take star sights using a sextant alongside in Bahrain meant I saw little of the Persian Gulf for quite a long time.

One evening as it was getting dark and we were on passage I was having an amble up the Iron Deck to towards the bows. As I approached the for'ard gun mountings I heard what sounded like an argument going on in the area between the gun mountings and the bow. Not wanting to intrude I peered around the gun mounting. Standing up in the bow was the large figure of a Royal Marine. He was leaning over the bow with something in his grip.

HMS ANZIO

Reproduced by permission of Imperial War Museum

On closer inspection this 'something' was another Royal Marine. From the ensuing conversation it appeared if suspended Marine did not agree with his companion he was going to be dropped into the sea. My thought processes said that if I intervene it is possible the suspended Marine will be dropped, I also had by now identified the pair; they were a couple of close pals known to everyone as Little and Large due to the difference in their sizes. If one was around almost certainly the other one was close by. I decided that it was unlikely that Large would drop Little and beat a retreat down the Iron Deck. However I did not go inboard until I saw the pair of them walking down the deck as though nothing had happened.

During my time in ANZIO I took a flight back to the UK from Bahrain for compassionate reasons. In 1962 the RAF had regular trooping flights to/from the Mid and Far East and the RAF section at RAF Muharraq was very efficient at getting me an early flight back to the UK. The first leg was from Bahrain to Aden. It just so happened that a new Argosy transport plane was carrying out hot weather trials in Bahrain and that night was due to fly to Aden. The Argosy was totally empty and I was given a seat, the only one, dead centre on the empty cargo deck. As the aircraft was on trials it was not allowed to fly direct to Aden across the Arabian desert but had to follow the coast, through the Hormuz Straits and thence to Aden. The result was a long hot flight of seven hours. On arrival in Aden I was put into the Red Sea Hotel, the RAF transit hotel, as my flight from Aden was not until the next day. I had a room with a small balcony overlooking the main street. That afternoon I sat idly watching the goings on and right beneath my balcony a cart carrying what looked like hay, drawn by a small donkey spontaneously burst into flames. That enlivened both my and the donkey's afternoon.

The following morning transport took me to RAF Khormaksar to catch the trooping flight coming through from Singapore and Gan. The arrivals and departure halls were not that big and were adjacent to one another. I was aware of a disturbance amongst the passengers disembarking from the Britannia as they came into the arrivals hall and there were some RAF Police in attendance. In order to accommodate me on the Britannia one of the passengers flying through to UK was having to be left in Aden to catch the next trooping flight. This would normally be a passenger who was taking up an 'indulgence' seat, (available to service men and women and their dependents using empty seats on a trooping flight). On my return to Bahrain some two weeks later I was to learn that the passenger selected was the wife of an Army Major returning to the UK from Singapore. Unfortunately for her she had been found to be running a brothel in Aden and had been very quickly removed to Singapore with the warning that if she ever set foot in Aden again she would be arrested and charged. Understandably she was upset at being removed from the flight. Whether or not she was arrested and charged I never did find out.

Having returned to ANZIO it was time for some rest and relaxation. Having disembarked the 17th/21st Lancers in Aden with their 8 tanks it was time for some relaxation.

Our Captain, Paddy McKeown, decided the Wardroom should visit the Tarshein Club, the Officers Club in Aden. When Paddy said 'we' he meant everyone. It was a fairly boozy evening and eventually the only people in the bar were the ANZIO Wardroom. Paddy for reasons best known to himself decided that he would walk down the length of the bar and kick the glasses off 'rugby style'. Within seconds the barman made it clear this was not welcome, demanded Paddy's ships name and said the Tarshein Club manager would be calling on the ship's captain the following morning. Paddy did not let on. The following morning as Officer of the Day I received a very poo faced civilian onboard who demanded to see the captain. I took him to Paddy's cabin, shut the door and left. Civilian manager left some 30 minutes later with a smile on his face. Paddy never disclosed what had been discussed.

ANZIO left Aden and proceeded down the East African coast to Mombasa. Mombasa had an RNLO (Royal Navy Liaison

Officer), but the post was due to be withdrawn shortly. We had been tasked with taking some transport, boats and furniture back up to Aden for shipment to the UK. We also had onboard an officer from 45 Cdo Royal Marines and two grooms based in Aden, whose job was to buy polo ponies for the Commando and we were to take them back to Aden.

ANZIO anchored in Kilindini Harbour and one of the first things the RNLO offered us was two Land Rovers, trailers and camping gear to go off into the Tsavo National Park for a short safari. Volunteers were quick in coming forward, myself included. Two days later we set off for the Tsavo National Park, an assorted group of Royal Marines and Ships Company. The Royal Marines being 'ruffy tuffy' took the lead and had identified a small mountain as the first objective within the park. Driving on rural Kenyan roads had not been allowed for and it was dark before we started the ascent of the 'small mountain' on a very dubious track. More by luck than judgement we reached what appeared to be the top. Everyone was knackered so it was a matter of putting up the tents, having a brew and getting our heads down for the remainder of the night.

When I awoke, it was light and I pulled across the tent entrance flap. What a sight. We had camped on a south facing slope and ahead of me all I could see was low cloud with the sun streaming down and in the distance some 40 miles away the snow covered cap of Kilimanjaro poking up through the sea of cloud into the clear blue sky. By now everyone was awake and even the ruffy tuffy Royal Marines were dumbstruck by the sight in front of us. The remainder of the trip is a bit of a haze apart from one incident when we met a lone large elephant on the road ahead. We had been warned that lone elephants tended to be male and dangerous. Both Land Rovers stopped and awaited the elephants next move. It did not appear unhappy with our presence and started walking in our direction. Making a quick reverse getaway was going to be made more difficult by the trailers so we sat tight. Unfortunately one of the younger Royal Marines in the rear Land Rover decided he would be safer in the African bush, leapt out of the Land Rover and disappeared. Happily the elephant decided to turn off the road and once we had rounded up our brave comrade we returned without further incident to Mombasa.

The trip from Mombasa to Aden was uneventful but I did learn that horses cannot be sea-sick. The polo ponies on the tank deck would go through the motions of being sea-sick but would never bring anything up. The grooms spent to lot of time with them on the tank deck.

Back in Aden we disembarked all the RNLOs gear and the 45 Cdo polo ponies and embarked the Royal Scots Greys, their tanks and their ammunition. One of my ancillary tasks was as the derrick loading officer (for want of a better word). ANZIO

HMS Anzio. Crossing the Line ceremony enroute to Mombasa. 1962

had two large stanchions through which steam driven winches manoeuvred a large hook for lifting and shifting cargo onboard. This was mainly tank gun ammunition which was stowed on the upper deck. Once I had mastered the technique of controlling the two steam winches by hand signals it became a matter of pride to ensure that every load coming inboard was in the right place first time.

We set off for Bahrain up the South Arabian coast. The Captain, Paddy McKeown was a Korean war veteran flying piston engine Sea Furys. Annually the Fleet Air Arm celebrate Taranto night and Paddy decided the Wardroom would celebrate Taranto night at sea on passage to Bahrain with the Royal Scots Greys in attendance. No one was excused attendance apart from the Officer of the Watch at the time. I was due for the Morning Watch from 0400 to 0800. As the only other Fleet Air Arm officer onboard I was expected to support Paddy throughout the dinner and beyond. At 0345 I left the celebrations a little bit worse for wear

HMS Anzio. Looking forward up the Iron Deck. 1962

HMS Anzio. Looking aft to the Quarterdeck. 1962

Ministry of Defence Crown copyright 1962

but I had, I thought, been quite careful in what I had drunk. I took over the watch up on the Flying Bridge (mounted between the stanchions mentioned earlier). The Quartermaster was in his wheel-house some 20 feet below the bridge. I checked the chart, looked around the horizon and saw a few tankers going about their lawful business. A brisk walk up and down the bridge and I sat down in the Captain's chair.

The next thing I knew a vibration had woken me. Where was I? What was happening? I looked from the Captain's Chair down the ladder to the Wheelhouse. Coming up was Paddy, still in his Mess Kit. Within seconds I was off the chair and trying to look alert. Paddy as garrulous as ever, wanted to know where we were, I pointed to the chart without a clue as to where we actually were, Paddy said that was OK, that he was not to be disturbed for the rest of the day and took his leave.

Once Paddy had negotiated the descent of the bridge ladder safely, I managed to pull myself together and went down to have words with the Quartermaster. It was 0730. The team in the wheelhouse were aware of the dinner! After I had failed to answer their calls for about thirty minutes one of them had come up to the bridge, looked at the chart which had a straight line on it for at the next eight hours of travel, and decided, as they had not altered course, they must be on the right track, so left me slumbering in the Captain's Chair. Who was I to argue with their logic! We arrived back in Bahrain safely.

ANZIO was planned to do a dry docking in Bombay as the watertight compartments in the hull were leaking. On the way to Bombay we visited Karachi. We held a cocktail party onboard. As the Wines and Spirits Officer I had to organise the bar etc. I needed ice for the drinks and spoke with the Pakistani Naval Liaison Officer. He was very helpful and we drove out to what appeared to be an ice making plant on the outskirts of Karachi and arranged for a dustbin sized ice block to be delivered to ANZIO. The cocktail party got underway and I noticed guests making a face on sipping their drinks. Having been busy ensuring all the arrangements were in place I had not yet taken a drink, but when I did I realised what the problem was. There was a distinctly 'fishy' taste and smell. A quick word with the Pakistani Navy Liaison Officer uncovered why. The ice making plant was in fact part of a fish processing plant. The ice was immediately ditched!

Our dry docking in Bombay was an interesting. Our Indian Navy Liaison Officer was Cdr Ginger. Walking up the jetty with him one day he was addressed by a number of dockyard workers in their own language. I asked what they had been saying and he replied he did not know as he only spoke English! We played the Indian Navy at cricket on one of the pitches in a public park in the heart of Bombay. Our first job was to clear the pitch of people sleeping on it. The minute we finished the game all the sleepers appeared and reclaimed their spaces. The Indian Navy invited us to their Officers Club on Marine Drive. It was a good evening until our hosts invited us into their brothel adjacent to the club at which point Paddy made our excuses and we all left. As Bombay State was a 'dry' state a licence was required to have a drink in an hotel. The licence had to be left with the security guard at the door and on buying your drink the bar tender would shout across what you had ordered and the guard marked it off your licence. There was a monthly limit. On entering a bar nearing the end of the month the guard would shout out to the assembled drinkers how much you had left on your licence so they could drink on what was left! We were taken on a tour of the Bombay night life from the Bombay Cages where people lived literally in cages with bars, to the most opulent brothels and everything in between. Bombay was a fascinating place and a real eyeopener.

The two words ANZIO and Bombay are synonymous with cockroaches. Every week in the Gulf there was a competition between the various messdecks to see who could get the most weight of cockroaches over the week. The messdeck with the most was awarded a cake! In my bunk in my non airconditioned cabin the cockroaches ran all over me during the night. The only respite was when it was extra hot and we all moved into the Wardroom, which was air-conditioned, with our mattresses – bliss. In Bombay they had a very large version of cockroaches known as the Bombay Runner. To say they were the size of small dogs is an exaggeration, but not far off. ANZIO had to put rat guards on all wires/ropes, not for the rats but against the cockroaches. They were plentiful in the dockyard and if you managed to stamp on one it exploded with a sharp crack. On leaving Bombay we were relieved that it appeared we had none on board. However, during one of my Middle Watches (0001-0400) going across the Arabian Sea I had the impression that something was on the guard rail; took the Aldis lamp out and shone it on the guard rail. Sure enough, there was a Bombay Runner scurrying along the rail. During succeeding night watches everyone saw this cockroach but it was never caught. If there was one there was probably more.

Our refit period in Bombay ended on a high. We were due to leave on a Monday. A crucial piece of engineering equipment had been flown out to us and our Indian Navy Liaison Officer established it had arrived in Bombay airport but the Indian Customs would not release it. It was Friday afternoon. The advice from the Liaison Officer was to go to the Customs main office in central Bombay and make a fuss. Every officer was rounded up and we set out for the Customs Office. The plan was to occupy the relevant offices and refuse to leave until the engineering part was cleared through the airport. And that is exactly what we did. The Customs building was huge, full of offices and large open spaces filled with desks and paper, paper stacked high in rows and rows. All our officers sat in offices whilst Chris the 6'7" OCRM and the Engineer Officer went around establishing where they could get the necessary clearance. We were there for hours until Chris appeared with the thumbs up and the Engineer Officer disappeared to the airport to collect his piece of equipment. How we did not get arrested I will never know.

Whilst alongside in Bahrain one of the favourite pastimes of many onboard was to drop a fishing line overboard in order to catch fish to enliven the daily menus. One morning I heard that the Quarterdeck Leading Hand, Leading Seaman Anders, had caught an exceptionally large Grouper. It had been placed on a Quarterdeck bollard and left there over lunchtime. After lunch I wandered down to the Quarterdeck as part of my daily ramblings around the ship. The Leading Seaman was very proud of his catch, which still perched on the bollard and was assumed to be dead. He showed me his catch and rattled his fork (everyone had their own eating irons about their person) inside its mouth. Instantly the Grouper snapped its mouth shut and beheaded his fork. Why I remember this incident and Leading Seaman Anders name is a mystery to me!

The Wardroom had its own team of Chefs and Stewards who all came from Goa. They provided an excellent service and excellent food. However they were not good sailors and if we met any rough seas they would be found huddled up in a corner suffering terribly from sea sickness. Consequently the standard of food relied upon the daily sea state!

I had my first encounter with death on Anzio. A young engineering Petty Officer joined the ship from the UK and went straight into watch keeping duties in the Boiler Room. He was overweight but not excessively so. One evening at sea just after he had arrived I met him in a passageway not looking at all well and sweating profusely. I helped him to the Sick Bay and called the doctor. Apparently his body temperature was off the clock and he was put into a bath of ice to cool him down. Later that night he passed away. A decision was made to bury the Petty Officer at sea and presumably this was agreed with his next of kin. The Coxswain had the job of making the sailcloth shroud and putting in the last stitch through the nose to ensure that he was indeed dead. It was a sombre couple of days onboard.

My seven months on Anzio were interesting and there are more stories, like the tug which capsized as it was towing us out of the dry dock, and that of VIKRANT (the Indian Navy aircraft carrier), which had been in the dry dock before us, which 'flooded up' with plates still missing under the waterline and hence had flooded compartments.

It was time to go back to Front Line flying. The Wessex HAS 1 had entered service and I was to return to RNAS Portland for Refresher Operational Flying and No 65 Anti-Submarine Operational Flying Training (OFT) course.

Chapter 5

HMS VICTORIOUS

814 Squadron/Wessex HAS 1.
August 1963 – September 1964

Before joining 814 Squadron I had to complete my refresher Operational Flying Training and qualify on the Wessex HAS 1.

The Whirlwind HAS 7 and Wessex HAS 1 were like chalk and cheese. The dipping sonar was the same as that of the Whirlwind, the Type 194. There was now a turbine engine powering the blades instead of the Whirlwind piston engine. Auto Stabilisation Equipment (ASE), meant that the aircraft, once trimmed out, could be flown 'hands off'. A Flight Control System (FCS) had been introduced. Once the aircraft had arrived at a 'gate' (90 ft; into wind; 125 ft) the FCS would automatically take the aircraft into a hover, and once the dipping sonar ball had been lowered would hold the aircraft in the hover at a predetermined height. Louis Newmark manufactured the ASE and FCS equipment, the first to be used in helicopters. They were simplex systems and were not fail safe. Many hours were spent simulating equipment failures as some could be quite dramatic. To find your aircraft suddenly deciding to fly backwards at 40 knots, at 40 feet, on a dark and stormy night, dragging the sonar ball through the water does nothing to improve your day. But, Anti-Submarine night flying had arrived. The Wessex HAS1 also had a dramatic improvement in speed, endurance and payload. A Whirlwind HAS7 could only carry either a torpedo or a dipping sonar - the Wessex could carry both.

Anti-Submarine operations involved detecting the submarine using the 'dipping sonar' of the helicopter. In the early days the short detection ranges of the helicopter sonar gave the submarine an advantage. However if there were two or three helicopters involved in the action with two in contact and the third moving to its next dipping position the advantage turned to the helicopter. The 'senior' helicopter - 'Observer' would take charge of the action, and in the event of losing contact would decide the best 'Airplan', a laid down sequence of events, to regain contact. The Observer was the tactical coordinator. Weapons available to the Observer to attack and sink or disable the submarine were torpedoes and depth charges. Navigating the Whirlwind whilst tracking submarines had been very much a matter of 'jumping' in the right direction and hoping the next 'dip' was in the place it intended to be. The experience of the Observer and coordination with the Pilot were critical. There were no aids for the pilot other than a dial which gave an indication of where the dipping sonar cable was in relation to the aircraft. The dial had two needles at right angles to each other. As long as the two needles remained central the hover position was correct and the sonar cable was vertical in the water. Aircraft height was measured by taking the depth of the sonar ball and the amount of cable out. The aircraft was very much in the manual mode and if it remained in the hover for 30 minutes that was 30 minutes of hard labour for the pilot. Leaving the hover could be exciting. If the sonar cable was being dragged forwards, backwards or sideways as it left the water it could induce a swing. To the pilot the sight of the sonar body appearing in his forward vision could be more than off putting. Anti-Submarine operations at night were not possible. Night flying was practised but it tended to be overland navigation exercises.

700(H) Squadron, the Wessex Intensive Flying Trials Unit had spent many hours in Falmouth Bay working on 'Jump Navigation' and produced a series of graph tables based on windspeed. Two sets, one half for manual jumping during daytime without the assistance of the FCS and the other half for night time jumping. With these graphs the accuracy in Jump Navigation improved dramatically. Navigation was no longer sticking your finger in the air.

Grenades were carried on Anti-Submarine exercises for communication to the submarine. For example two grenades indicated COMEX, commencement of the exercise. During forward flight the Whirlwind could be trimmed out which could leave the pilot with a spare hand. There were many occasions when the Observer or Aircrewman would indicate they had something for the pilot. On putting his hand down under the seat the 'something' would turn out to be a grenade with the pin out!

814 Squadron embarked in HMS VICTORIOUS which had just completed a refit (which included air conditioning throughout) and we set sail for the Far East. It was planned to be a relatively fast passage to the Far East, working up the Air Group enroute. VICTORIOUS passed through the Suez Canal which was enlivened by the appearance of the 'gully gully' men onboard. These are Egyptian 'magicians' who earned their living by performing tricks onboard ships passing up and down the canal. They specialised in producing live chickens from under miniature hats! The Egyptian Air Force also put on a show for as we passed one of their air force bases lining the canal. A fighter jet with the pilot presumably looking at VICTORIOUS as she passed, crashing into the runway and burst into flames.

VICTORIOUS made a detour before crossing the Indian Ocean to Dar-as-Salem. On 13 August I was the Duty Officer attending the departure of Captain Peter Compston, Captain of VICTORIOUS in one of our aircraft, to a VIP lunch ashore. The Captain was dressed in his best white unform complete with sword and medals. As Lieutenant Mike Holcroft pulled in the power to take off there was an explosion and flames from the engine area. The engine had shed its turbine blades. Within seconds there was a cloud of white acrid smoke enveloping the aircraft. The fire fighters were in immediately. The first person to exit the cabin door was Captain Compston and by now his immaculate white uniform had turned a shade of grey. However he retained his composure and remarked to me, whilst passing, that maybe he would not be travelling in that particular aircraft today.

Throughout the outgoing voyage which ended in a visit to Hong Kong there were frequent exercises to cover all emergencies. There were also a number of real emergencies, mainly small fires, which had to be dealt with. By the time VICTORIOUS arrived in Hong Kong the ships company were well exercised.

Lieutenant Commander 'Tommy' Denholm was our Air Engineering Officer. A real Fleet Air Arm character. Tommy was into jazz and to his delight Kenny Ball and his Jazzmen were performing in Hong Kong. He got a ticket, got backstage, met Kenny Ball and being Tommy invited the band to lunchtime drinks onboard. As a squadron we hosted them in the Wardroom. To get to the Wardroom there were three sets of ladders to descend plus corridors to navigate, so you feel you are in the bowels of the ship. There we were, the squadron plus Kenny Ball and his five jazzmen, having a few pints at lunchtime. Over the Ships Broadcast 'FIRE, FIRE, FIRE, fire in such and such a compartment'. Conversation stopped, one officer shot across the Wardroom and exited at speed. Nobody else moved. Conversations resumed. Had we not been hearing this for the past two months? However, if you are not familiar with the procedure, down in what appears to be the bowels of a ship on fire, with no one apparently caring whether you survive or not, then that is different. The effect upon Kenny Ball and his Jazzmen was dramatic. They froze, looked around nervously, and their voices went up an octave. This effect went on for a couple of minutes until we realised how they felt and gave them reassurance that they were unlikely to die in the next few minutes!

In Hong Kong, races from the bar of the Mandarin Hotel to the bar of the Hilton Hotel were legendary. Both bars were located on their top floors and were within sight of each other. Both buildings were tall and stood out from other buildings on Hong

Kong island. (During my last visit to Hong Kong in the mid 90's it was difficult to find the Mandarin/Hilton as they were dwarfed by the vast skyscrapers now dominating the landscape.) The record was around 10 minutes. 'Liberating' a life-size plus wooden figure of a Viking (one of two) from outside an hotel in Kowloon was planned by the Squadron - we needed it as a mascot. However the subsequent chase through the streets and ultimate ditching of the figure into the harbour put paid to the mascot idea. A good run ashore normally started with a line of us singing the High Ho song from Snow White and the Seven Dwarfs as we made our way through the Kowloon streets, one foot in the gutter, and the other on the pavement, on the way to our squadron bar. The callowness of youth!!

One lunchtime Angus Suggit, Chris Hodgkinson and I decided to go ashore and each get a tattoo. No alcohol involved, stone cold sober. We found a tattoo parlour and I ended up going first and getting a small dragon tattoo on my wrist. I emerged with a bandage over the tattoo and according to Angus and Chris my face was ashen. It had been painful, but not that painful. Both declined to get their tattoo!

On the 22 November 1963 my logbook shows I took off at 1900 for a 2 hour anti-submarine sortie in the South China Sea off the Philippines. At around 2130 I was back in the Air Crew Refreshment Bar (ARCB) enjoying a bacon roll or two when the news came though that President Kennedy had been shot dead in Dallas. A moment never to be forgotten.

Christmas was spent disembarked at RNAS Sembawang.

In January 1964 there was considerable unrest in East Africa. Zanzibar had been granted complete independence from Britain on 10 December 1963 and on 12 January 1964 rebels in Zanzibar had begun a bloody revolt to declare a republic. Naval units were put on standby but the British High Commissioner did not request evacuation of British citizens as many key government posts were still held by British citizens and sudden removal could have disrupted the country's economy and government. On 19 January 700 men of the 1st Battalion Tanganyika Rifles mutinied against their white British officers and briefly took control of the capital Das-Es-Salem. On 25 January similar mutinies were taking place and HMS CENTAUR landed 45 Commando and the rebels surrendered within 24 hours. VICTORIOUS had been called upon as a reinforcement. On 27 January at midday along with a Supply Officer I was landed at Port Reitz airfield, Mombasa's airfield. The Supply Officer had the ship's Malaysian/Singapore currency, and we expected a Gannet in from CENTAUR with all their East African currency so that a swop could be effected. For reasons which I do not remember the Supply Officer made a phone call and then disappeared into Mombasa. The Port Reitz terminal consisted of a very small wooden building with a large raised veranda out front. This building had everything from arrivals, departures, air traffic control, ticket sales and café facilities. So I sat on my ownsome on the veranda with thousands of pounds worth of Malaysian/ Singapore currency wondering if it was worth buying a ticket to somewhere exotic. Within 30 minutes the Gannet arrived, we swopped currency bags, and the Gannet left. I now had thousands of pounds worth of East African currency in my possession and I felt slightly vulnerable as I eyed the locals who were coming and going into the terminal. At 1530 the Supply Officer returned with a grin on his face and at 1600 we were collected to fly back to VICTORIOUS.

VICTORIOUS anchored in Kilindini Harbour on the 27 January, CENTAUR arrived on 28 January and we transferred some equipment/ stores and personnel and embarked two Belvederes. We sailed on 29 January and my logbook shows that we began embarking 45 Commando from Dar es Salem on 30 January. Where do you put the Royal Marines of 45 Commando on an already crowded carrier? The photo on the accompanying page shows you. On 4 February Lieutenant Al Rock and I flew Tanganyikan Ministers from VICTORIOUS to the Das es Salem

HMS Centaur passing HMS Victorious on arrival in Kilindini Harbour, Mombasa. January 1963

Ministry of Defence Crown Copyright 1963

Gymkhana Club. But it was back to business on 5 February as I was wet winching 801 Squadron aircrew out of the Indian Ocean.

From 9 – 22 February I embarked on HMS ALBION with an 814 Squadron detachment to assist in an amphibious exercise off Malindi Beach north of Mombasa.

By mid-Summer 1964 HMS Victorious was in an extended Maintenance Period in Singapore. 814 Squadron had disembarked to RNAS Sembawang for the period.

In Borneo 845 Squadron (Wessex HU5) was looking for an Observer to relieve their Operations Officer at Sibu (HMS Hornbill) in order that he might return to the UK for some well-

Cross-decking by RAF Belvederes from HMS Centaur to HMS Victorious. 1963

Where do you accommodate visitors unexpected visitors? In the hangar!. 1963

HMS Victorious Replenishing At Sea (RAS). Note 2 x RAF Belvederes at backend of Flight Deck. 1963

Ministry of Defence Crown Copyright 1963

earned leave. 845 Squadron were providing helicopter support in the Sarawak 3rd Division during the Borneo Confrontation with Indonesia. I volunteered having enjoyed the experience of the amphibious exercises earlier in the year.

The journey to Sibu was via an RAF Hastings from RAF Changi to Kuching (Borneo) followed by a Borneo Airways Dakota to Sibu. This second flight was enlivened by a variety of passengers including chickens and goats.

Sibu was the main operating base for 845 Squadron in the Sarawak 3rd Division with a detachment at a Forward Operating Base (FOB) at Nanga Gaat some 120 miles up country near to the Indonesian border. A quick handover and I settled down for the next few weeks which would be spent between Sibu and Nanga

Gaat. Tasks included running the Ops Room and acting as an Aircrewman when necessary.

One of my early sorties was a Resupply Flight out of Nanga Gaat. The resupply was to an SAS patrol 'somewhere' in the Borneo jungle. Apart from the supplies there was one SAS passenger, Major Pat Beresford. Following the descent through the trees into a jungle clearing our passenger disappeared into the undergrowth and we sat 'burning and turning' waiting for his return. I became aware that in the trees and undergrowth at the edge of the clearing were people, quite small people, with not many clothes on. They watched us from the shadows. Eventually the Major returned and sat in the rear of the cabin of the aircraft writing in his notebook. We took off vertically and the moment we got above the jungle canopy we hit wind-shear and the aircraft veered unexpectedly to port. Major Beresford who would have experienced quite a violent shock sitting in the tail of the aircraft did not even look up from his writing. I was to later learn that the small naked people I had seen in the clearing were members of the Punan tribe. As a post-script to that memory, the death of Lord Patrick Beresford was announced on 18 June 2020, which took me back immediately to that take-off in the middle of 'somewhere'.

A second Resupply Flight to an SAS patrol 'somewhere' in the 'ulu' (jungle) involved picking up an injured SAS team member. As time on the ground was critical resupply was normally a matter of dropping the rations, swopping the patrol's rum ration for beer (they preferred beer) and leaving quickly. This time we also had an injured team member, who was obviously in a lot of pain as he was screaming, literally thrown into the aircraft, followed by a rapid take-off. The team member had a back injury and was immediately casevac'd back to British Military Hospital Singapore. I was able to visit him weeks later in the hospital where he made a good recovery.

I spent quite a lot of time up at Nanga Gaat, the squadron's Forward Operating Base (FOB), complete with the Anchor Inn. In the photo accompanying this page Gurkhas of the 1st Battalion of

Gurkha troops emplaning into 845 Squadron Wessex HU5 at Nanga Gaat, a Forward Operating Base (FOB) in Sarawak. 1963

Ministry of Defence Crown Copyright 1963

the 6th Queen Elizabeth Own Gurkha Rifles are seen emplaning on the upper site prior to an operational mission. Lights out at 1030 when the generator shut down. During one of my overnight stops, just after midnight, there was the sound of gunfire from the perimeter. The firing had come from the detachment of Royal Irish Rangers (RIR) who had the responsibility of guarding the FOB. The imperative now was to get the three aircraft at Nanga Gaat out of the FOB and back to Sibu. I manned an aircraft on the Upper Site in the left hand seat with Lieutenant John Nicholls, waiting for the signal to start up and go.

Suddenly the aircraft rocked gently and there was a figure quietly climbing up the side of the aircraft. Luckily for the 'aircraft maintainer', for that is who it was, and for me, the safety catch on my Sterling was 'off'. The maintainer informed us the decision had

Nanga Gaat High Site. 1963

Ministry of Defence Crown Copyright 1963

Aerial view of Nanga Gaat Forward Operating Base in Sarawak. 1963

Ministry of Defence Crown Copyright 1963

been made by the RIR detachment commander to get the aircraft out immediately. At 0315 we took off and headed up through the clouds and westwards to Sibu. During the silent hours there was no radio contact maintained between Nanga Gaat and Sibu so they would not be aware that we were on our way. The cloud cover was continuous and it was only by dead reckoning that we would arrive over Sibu. Ninety minutes later we arrived over what I hoped was Sibu Airport. A skeleton staff of maintainers was kept at the airport overnight and quick thinking by the team, who had heard the aircraft and put two and two together, enabled them to get a vehicle onto the runway and use the lights to guide us in. As we neared the coast the cloud had thinned and we saw the vehicle lights through the clouds. The plan was to return to Nanga Gaat at daybreak with reinforcements.

However reinforcements were not required! The RIR had recently assumed the task of guarding Nanga Gaat from the Gurkhas. There were rumours that there had been a massacre of Japanese soldiers during WW2 at Nanga Gaat and ghosts were occasionally seen in the area. During the night movement had been seen which had led to the gunfire. At daybreak the 'movement' had been found to be a cow owned by the locals. The cow was deceased. Some Squadron maintainers could not resist finding another cow and painting in large white letters the word COW on its side, just to make a point. Life was never dull at Nanga Gaat - the first time the RIR 'stood to' in their trenches dug by the Gurkhas they found out the average RIR was somewhat larger than the average Gurkha!

The day after the COW incident we received a call in the Sibu Ops Room requesting assistance in transporting a woman who had been in labour for a number of days from her Dyak village, Mukam, some 40 miles away and take her to Sibu Hospital. I went along as navigator/extra eyes. All went well, the lady was delivered to the hospital giving birth shortly afterwards (the helicopter ride had had the right effect). A cutting from *Flight* magazine reported the incident a few months later commenting that the baby had been named 'helicopter'!

There was a task to get mail up to Nanga Gaat, but I had no serviceable aircraft available at Sibu. The Army Air Corps had an Auster based at Sibu and Sgt Thackeray volunteered to fly the mail up. He had to complete some practice landings at Kapit airstrip and would drop the mail first. With no airstrip at Nanga Gaat it would have to be an Air Drop. I went along to act as his Despatcher. Once over Nanga Gaat it was obvious we could not do the drop on either the Upper or Lower sites as there were aircraft on the pads. The only other option was a strip of clear ground between the River Rajang and the accommodation. The receiving ground party moved into place, a practice pass and then the Air Drop. A final pass and the ground party were all waving happily. We went onto Kapit and returned to Sibu. On return to

A young happy beardless Operations Officer in Borneo

News item regarding new arrival in the world

Sibu there were a number of very rude messages in from Nanga Gaat. Apparently I had managed to drop the mail straight into the Rajang. The happily waving ground party were actually shaking their fists at the inept mail drop!

Gulong Spali was a 3000ft mountain which on a good day could be seen from Sibu Airport. The Army had a listening post atop the mountain but for reasons best known to them it was to be abandoned. Most of the kit and people had been ferried back and there was one last load of four people. My 'old and bold' pilot and I took off at 1400 to carry out the last sortie. The landing site was on a ledge above a 1000ft cliff and on arrival we found that instead of 4 people there were eight and they still had some equipment. A few calculations proved that we would be well overweight which would mean another sortie to clear the site. My 'old and bold' pilot reckoned if we loaded everyone with the aircraft close to the edge and we did a 'jump take-off', and used the 1000ft to gain speed then we would be OK and save the extra trip. To someone with an Anti-Submarine Warfare background where power margins and AUWs (All Up Weight) were important, this sounded like madness. But he was convincing and moments later as we began the long descent (falling like a stone) towards the point at which we had enough airspeed to begin to level out. I began to question my sanity. We all lived to tell the tale!

61

Wessex HU Mk 5 undercarriage damaged in a landing near the Indonesian border being repaired at Sibu Airport. 300lb undercarriage unit was removed, repaired, and replaced in 8 minutes. 1965

Ministry of Defence Crown Copyright 1965

One afternoon at Nanga Gaat I and some other new arrivals were invited to visit a Dyak Long House further up the River Rajang. The detachment had made friends with the Dyaks by inviting them to the Anchor Inn on occasion and from time to time the Dyaks reciprocated. Transport was provided by a long slender canoe-like craft with an outboard engine. It was an exciting ride being so close to the water at what felt like breakneck speed. Our group was welcomed into the Long House which to my mind was just like the films! Up rickety steps into the gloom and then we all sat around drinking tuak the local wine made from fermented rice. We were shown some shrunken heads and assured that they were not recent and were very old. Conversation was conducted in 'pidgin english' as none of us spoke Iban! Tuak is apparently not that strong but I do not remember much about the boat ride back. Must have been something I ate.

One thing I did not collect was a Dyak tattoo. They are applied using a nail through a stick which is dipped in a black liquid and the nail applied to your skin and hit with a stone. It is extremely painful, but that did not stop a lot of detachment members obtaining one. It did provide a steady revenue steam for the tattooer.

The next three stories are connected to the RAF. They all happened as described and were amusing at the time and therefore worth recounting. There has always been a rivalry between the Fleet Air Arm and the RAF but there is also respect; we just have different rules to follow.

In the Ops Room we received a tasking message requesting an aircraft to assist in looking for a suitable Air Defence Radar (ADR) site in our area. On the appointed day a Squadron Leader arrived with his umbrella and a map of the proposed reconnaissance area. The map of the area showed a lot of white areas surrounded by high ground where, in theory, an ADR could be situated. The white areas were in fact areas that had not yet been mapped and were like the rest of Borneo, full of valleys and mountains, resembling a wrinkled prune. The Squadron Leader was not convinced and demanded to be flown over the area just to make sure. My logbook shows a three hour reconnaissance flight, but does not mention an increasingly frustrated Squadron Leader. Regrettably the Squadron Leader had not endeared himself to the Ops Room staff with the result that they spent some time manufacturing 'confetti' and whilst we were away on his flight concealing the confetti within his umbrella.

An RAF VIP was scheduled to fly up to Nanga Gaat to inspect the facilities available in the event that the RN pulled out of Borneo and the RAF had to take over the facility. An RAF Whirlwind 10 had pre-positioned from Labuan complete with VIP qualified pilot to carry out the flight to Nanga Gaat. RAF VIP arrives, his 'aide' checks the VIP license category and discovers that the Whirlwind 10 pilot is not qualified to carry his VIP. The 'aide' arrives in the Ops Room and asks if we have an aircraft that could do the Nanga Gaat trip. Two weeks previously a Sub Lieutenant pilot, straight from training, had arrived from the UK and had completed his familiarisation flight up to Nanga Gaat the previous week. The weather was good and the forecast was good. The route to Nanga Gaat was straightforward and there was an aircraft available. The Sub Lieutenant was briefed, the RAF VIP and 'aide' did not ask for the pilot's credentials and away they went. The party returned later that day satisfied with their visit, said thank you, and left. I rest my case on rules.

And finally it was time to return to 814 Squadron in RNAS Sembawang. Borneo Airways to Kuching but no goats this time. I join a motley crew of Army, RN and RAF personnel for the flight back to RAF Changi in an RAF Argosy. Argosy appears, we all embark, preparing to leave the chocks, and there was a thunderous banging on the rear personnel door next to where I was sitting. There was a shouted conversation between the Loadmaster and someone outside followed by the engines shutting down, the doors opening, and we were all invited to leave the aircraft. There followed an animated conversation between one of the RAF passengers and one of the Argosy flight crew, a Flight Lieutenant. Minutes later the Flight Lieutenant started circulating amongst the passengers. The Argosy had been carrying out other tasks before taking us back to RAF Changi and was due to refuel at Kuching. Somehow the crew had 'forgotten' to refuel and it was only the intervention of the ground crew that had reminded them. The senior RAF passenger had 'suggested' to the aircraft Captain, a Flight Lieutenant that he should personally apologise to every passenger for this oversight and delay. Red faces all round. We eventually arrived at RAF Changi somewhat late, but safe. On 14 October 2010 I was presented with the Pingat Jasa Malaysia medal by the Malaysian Defence Attache for my very small part in upholding Malaysian sovereignty during the Borneo Confrontation.

One skill that I did acquire during long sea passages without any flying was that of Bridge. The CO was Lieutenant Commander John Beyfus, rumoured to be a relation of Beyfus QC. One of his passions was Bridge which he used to pay off his monthly mess bill. The Wardroom had a 'Bridge Book' into which winnings and losses could be recorded. The sum being added/deducted from the next month's mess bill. Somehow I was sucked into playing Bridge and quite often ended up with John Beyfus as my partner. Not that he was all that pleased. He described my method of playing as 'Milne's Muddle'. Well it may have been a muddle at times, but he continued to pay off his mess bill through the Bridge Book so my playing cannot have been that bad.

Apart from learning Bridge, how did aircrew occupy themselves at sea in between periods of flying? A non-flying day would normally begin with Shareholders. At 0830 all aircrew would gather in the squadron Briefing Room and either the Senior Observer or Senior Pilot would conduct proceedings. This could range from 'brickbats' to 'bouquets'; updates on forthcoming exercises; briefing by a specialist; reminder that log books were due for their monthly signing; important notices etc etc. It was also useful to see that everyone was up and about! During the day there may be all-ship events such as going to Action Stations, and Damage Control Exercises rehearsing the whole ship reaction to an emergency. There would be specialist briefings given by the Qualified Helicopter Instructor (QHI) whose responsibility was keeping squadron flying standards high, or the Helicopter Warfare Instructor (HWI) whose responsibility was keeping the squadron up to date in the tactical use of the aircraft and weapons. The Meteorology Officer would give specialist briefings on the weather and on oceanography. Aircrew need to keep up to date with engineering procedures and documentation and there would be QS (Qualified to Sign for the Aircraft) lectures, practicals and examinations. Both Observers and Pilots would be Divisional Officers for the aircraft engineers and supply ratings (chefs, stewards and logistics) which meant writing regular reports on their Division, acting as their advice in disciplinary matters.

All Divisional work meant keeping in touch with their Division through personal contact and talking to their line managers. How Divisional Officers performed would be taken into account in their 'oily Qs',(- that is their Officer Like Qualities (OLQs)), when the squadron 'Wheels' came to write their reports. Some aircrew, to increase their Naval knowledge would undertake Bridge Watchkeeping. On a regular basis the squadron would be visited by the Naval Helicopter Flying Standards Flight – the 'Trappers'. The role of the NHSF was to check that the standard of flying and aircrew knowledge was the same high standard across the Fleet Air Arm. They would arrive on a planned basis but there was nothing

HMS Victorious and INS Vikrant (foreground) cooperating during a JET exercise. 1964

Ministry of Defence Crown Copyright 1964

814 Squadron Wessex HAS 1 being Counted Out and Counted In. 1964

Ministry of Defence Crown Copyright 1964

HMS Victorious carrying out Jackstay Transfer with a River Class frigate of the Australian Navy. 1964

Ministry of Defence Crown Copyright 1964

to stop them arriving unplanned. In the run up to a visit there would be additional briefings and lectures to ensure aircrew were up to standard. The Trappers would attend briefings and lectures, fly on sorties and interview crews and individuals. Their report would ultimately reflect the standard of the squadron and they had the right to recommend downgrading aircrew qualifications and categories. Exploring the ship was encouraged! It was surprising how many routes could be used to get from your cabin to the briefing room. Knowledge of the ship could be a lifesaver in the event of an emergency situation. Finding yourself in the Chinese Laundry in the bowels of the ship was an experience not to be forgotten.

The Chinese laundrymen or, 'dhobi wallahs', in naval parlance, deserve a book of their own. Traditionally the Dhobi are washer men, derived from the Hindu 'dhona' – to wash. Up until the late 1950s/early 60s laundry services in RN ships were provided by RN personnel who undertook the Laundry Course at HMS Drake. With ships spending long commissions in the Far East it was found that locally enlisted Chinese personnel were providing excellent laundry services. They cost nothing as they made their money from charging for their laundry services. Overtime the Chinese laundrymen provided a laundry service to all Royal Navy warships frigate and above. In major warships you would also find a Chinese cobbler and a tailor. The laundrymen lived in the bowels of the ship and catered for themselves. They lived in the laundry and literally slept on ironing boards. Although they were on the 'Ships Book' as crew they were not paid by the RN. They would be awarded military medals the same as the crew following operations. Laundrymen were contracted through Hong Kong businessmen and there was never any shortage of volunteers. As Second Officer of the Watch on the Forward Brow on a first day alongside in Sembawang Naval Dockyard I watched a large Rolls Royce draw up at the bottom of the gangway. Within minutes a very smartly dressed No 1 laundryman emerged from a hatch and walked down to the waiting Rolls. I do not remember having any complaints with the service apart from once having too much starch in my ceremonial white uniform jacket which buttoned up around my neck. To look around I had to physically move my body and looking down or up was impossible! I understand that since Hong Kong was handed back to China the situation has changed dramatically and there are no longer Chinese laundrymen on RN ships.

Whilst the ship was at sea one officer had an important job, the Line Book Officer (LBO). All squadrons had a Line Book which was a humorous account of life in the squadron, in particular with regard to runs ashore or flying incidents. The LBO was normally chosen for his artistic ability in cartoon drawing but he could use the skills of any other officer or use photographs, cut-outs from newspapers or magazines or anything thought appropriate. The Line Book could make fun of anyone or anything and was not designed to be malicious. Line Books would be put into the Wardroom as soon as the ship left harbour and would be removed in anticipation of a port visit. Line Books remained with their squadrons until they were disbanded when they were sent to the Fleet Air Arm Museum at Yeovilton.

Then there was the bathythermograph saga. A bathythermograph is a small torpedo shaped device containing a temperature sensor and a transducer to detect changes in the water temperature versus depth down to approximately 935 feet. Water temperature changes are very important to submarines and submarine hunters alike. Abrupt changes in water temperature can result in 'layers' where a submarine can hide, provided the dipping sonar is above or below the layer. If the dipping sonar body is in the layer it can enhance the chance of submarine detection. In order to get accurate data the bathy should be lowered straight down. The squadron had a bathy winch with 1000 ft of cord to which the bathy was attached. The winch was 'aircrew powered' so a member of the backseat crew would have the unenviable task of lowering the bathy and then winding it in again. This was real hot and sticky work and avoiding having to do the daily dip was great sport. It got to the state where I spoke with a Leading Airman (no names, no pack drill, but he knows who he is!) with whom I played rugby, to the effect that the entire squadron would be grateful if the bathy winch accidently fell over the side into the deepest part of the ocean. One dark and stormy night it disappeared.

There were times of course when everything got on top of people and there was a need to get away, pause, think, and reassemble your thoughts. There were places on most ships where this was possible, various sponsons, gangways, the flight deck, the chapel and the Quarterdeck. To take a book up and sit on a grating, reading, looking over the water can be very calming. Many a time I would sit and just watch the waves and the wake and not be conscious of other people who were around me doing exactly the same.

Rough weather was almost hypnotic but did not have a very calming effect. One day in the Mediterranean in a very violent storm to the West of Corsica remains a vivid memory. I was in Flyco watching the weather as VICTORIOUS was slowly running before the storm. The seas were monstrous. The Captain came through to discuss the situation with Cdr(Air) and it was decided we had to turn around otherwise we would end up on a Corsican beach. A slight increase in speed and we turned across sea, there was one mighty roll and the angled flight deck cut through the sea which by now was some hundreds of feet beneath us. Everyone in Flyco was hanging onto whatever they could find. There was crashing and banging all around as loose articles became flying articles. For seconds time was suspended until the angled flight deck emerged and VICTORIOUS rolled slowly in the opposite direction. The relief in Flyco and the Bridge was obvious. That was a truly scary moment for all watching it.

Mail was an important part of life onboard. Both the receipt and despatch of letters and parcels was watched with anticipation. At times it seemed remarkable that we received mail as it came from the most unlikely places. The British Forces Post Office did an exceptional job in keeping the flow going.

Mail would be collected from out of the way airfields as we passed by, from frigates or destroyers joining as our escort, from Royal Fleet Auxiliaries as we refuelled and resupplied, and from foreign and Naval Dockyards as we arrived. Mail was a priority and on one sortie from RNAS Sembawang we had to pick up both Flag Officer 2nd in Command of the Far East Fleet, (Vice Admiral Scratchard, known as 'Black Jack'), and the mail and return to Victorious. Unusually we shut down on the flight deck before disembarking our VIP. The Admiral left the aircraft to be welcomed by the Captain at which point I threw out the first heavy mail bag. Unfortunately the Admiral and the Captain had decided to chat just outside the cabin door and my first mail bag hit the quite short Admiral where his head met his shoulders and felled him to the deck. The Mail Party were more concerned with retrieving the mail bag than a downed Admiral.

Most aircrew did keep themselves gainfully occupied during the working day. Come the evening it would be meeting in the bar, followed by dinner, sometimes a Mess Dinner to celebrate Trafalgar Day or Taranto followed by games, inevitably squadron versus squadron, which would go on into the night. Once a week it would be film night. The film would be shown in the Wardroom bar area so the bar would be shut. Due to the space available the bar would form part of the seating. Film night always started with a Tom & Jerry type cartoon and at the end when the credits announced the Producer as 'Fred Quimpy' there would be a combined shout of 'Good Old Fred' - Why? Goodness only knows. All film projectors were old and infirm and there were frequent pauses where rectification work had to be done. Occasionally some brave squadron officer would approach the Film Officer and organise the projector and film or a private showing in the squadron briefing room. I remember watching the then very bawdy film 'Tom Jones' for the first time in a briefing room and almost collapsing from too much laughter.

Volunteers were required to attend the two week RAF Jungle Survival Course at RAF Changi on Singapore Island, two from each Squadron and two ship's officers. Chris Quarrie and I put our names forward and found ourselves selected along with the ship's Principal Medical Officer (PMO) and the Carrier Borne Ground Liaison Officer (CBGLO) an Army officer who was commonly known as 'Seaballs'. The first week of the course was spent in the classroom with a day going through a Singapore swamp and where we met Sun Bears. We learnt about jungle navigation, what to eat (and not to eat) and how to make shelters, which prepared us for the second week in the Malayan jungle.

Primary forest is forest which has not been disturbed by man and is easy to move through. Secondary forest is 'disturbed' forest which is very difficult to move through. Our week would be through a mixture of types. The course which had RN, RAF and Army personnel on it was divided into small groups for the first couple of days, then pairs for two days, then on your own. On the first nights having achieved our objective, constructed our 'bashas', and eaten something indescribable, the group would sit down around a fire and swop stories until turning in. Our Seaballs had served in Malaya during the Malayan Campaign against the terrorists and on the second night recounted some of his experiences in ambush positions. The story which made the biggest impression on us all was that whilst sitting in an ambush position he would get the feeling of being watched. On looking around he would espy an elephant literally feet away just standing watching. These were not isolated incidents but experienced generally by troops operating in the jungle. These Malayan elephants were quite small and moved through the jungle silently. They would watch and then move away as quietly as they came. As can be imagined we spent a lot of time looking into the 'ulu' imagining elephants there. Needless to say we never saw any. The last couple of nights were spent on our own (but within earshot of another course member). The other 'nugget' dropped by Seaballs was on snakes. Snakes are very partial to warmth and given the chance will slide in next to a warm body. Snakes can also detect heat and can jump. One of the methods of sleeping we had to practise was slinging a parachute silk between two trees to act as a hammock. Snakes had been known to leap into hammocks! The last two nights were spent mostly awake with minds racing! On the last day the entire course met up and started the walkout. At least we were now on a jungle track and the group snaked its way through the jungle. We came to a halt for no apparent reason, until back came the word 'tiger'. The front of the column had come across a tiger and cubs walking up the track, luckily in the same direction. Nobody had mentioned tigers during the first week, but we now knew why the instructors all carried a small arm during this phase.

Life as Officer of the Watch on the For'ard Brow was normally quite busy and there were always things in which you got involved and learnt from as described in my earlier story about

VICTORIOUS. Life as Officer of the Watch on the After Brow was a bit more staid. There was less going on, but you had to keep an eye on ceremonial; ships arriving and leaving, and generally it was a little bit boring compared to the For'ard Brow. On occasion it did get interesting. During a Middle Watch (0000 – 0400) whilst alongside in Singapore with HMS Cavalier (a 'C' Class Destroyer) astern of Victorious I became aware of an unusual amount of noise coming from the bow of Cavalier. A few minutes later there appeared to be people going down the brow of Cavalier and heading in the direction of Victorious After brow. Seconds later a naked man sped up my gangway and disappeared through one of the Quarterdeck doors. I sent the Bosun's Mate to chase him and the Quartermaster down the gangway to find out what was happening on Cavalier. The Bosun's Mate returned to say he had lost the naked man and the Quartermaster came back to report

814 Squadron 1964

Ministry of Defence Crown Copyright 1964

HMS Victorious ceremonial entry into Hong Kong. 1964

Ministry of Defence Crown Copyright 1964

that nobody on the Cavalier would tell him what had been going on. Part of the Duty Watch were called out to search for the naked man. By the time I handed over the Watch at 0400 he still had not been found. The next morning I caught up with the news. There had been a small party going on below decks in Cavalier and the result was that those present decided to hang the First Lieutenant from one of the barrels of the For'ard gun turret. Apparently the First Lieutenant was not too popular onboard. Those involved had managed to get the First Lieutenant to the gun turret but he had broken free and made his dash for freedom along the jetty to Victorious. Nobody on Cavalier ever admitted to being involved in such goings on and I believe the matter was dropped.

Everything happens in the Middle Watch! It was near Christmas and it was a quiet night. Out of the warm night air I hear the skirl of the pipes. It sounded like they came from the jetty so I had a walk around. The pipes continued but now they were coming from the flight deck. I took a walk up to the flight deck and here was a young air mechanic from one of the fixed wing squadrons playing his heart out marching up and down. In the still night with a slight breeze taking some of the heat away it was magic to hear the pipes, and I stood for some time just listening. Eventually he realised I was watching and stopped and we got into conversation. He loved his pipes and took them everywhere with him. Unfortunately his messmates would not let him practise on the messdeck – for understandable reasons, and the only time and place he got to practise were in the small hours on the fight deck. Total and absolute magic.

VICTORIOUS completed her Maintenance Period in Singapore and we left for Australia. On 31 August our Australian Navy exchange officer, Lt Zork Rorsheim, and I flew into Geraldton, North of Perth, to collect the press and TV crews prior to our arrival in Perth the next day. We landed on the Australian Rules Football ground and were greeted by the Mayor of Geraldton in his Parlour overlooking the ground. Lt Rorsheim had not been back to Australia for some time. It was hot and the mayor brought out some cool Swan Lager to celebrate Lt Rorsheim's return to his homeland; we sank a couple or three.

The press/TV were late and I distinctly remember standing with the fire extinguisher at the ready (AVPIN fires were well known) and wondering if I was steady enough to use it. The hour long return flight was completed without incident with my very happy Australian friend up front singing various Australian ditties to himself.

The squadron had made friends with an Australian SAS (Special Air Service) unit whilst in Singapore and a group of us were invited to a day with the Perth contingent at their 'headquarters'. Hiring a car, half a dozen of us drove out to the HQ address which turned out to be a nondescript bungalow literally in the middle of nowhere. Scrub and desert were all around. It was around 1000 and the place appeared to be deserted. Entering the bungalow was straight out of a film. Bodies lying everywhere, overturned chairs and general chaos. I never did get the full story, but it appears some SAS 'oppos' had driven from the other side of Australia, arrived late last night, and in true Aussie style they all had a few 'tinnies' which went on through the night until breakfast. I cannot remember what we did with the rest of the day!

The time came to return from Perth to Singapore. The Borneo Confrontation was continuing and Sukarno, the Indonesian leader, let it be known that the VICTORIOUS Task Group (six warships and three support ships) was not to return to Singapore via the straits between the islands of Sumatra and Java and if they did would be attacked. At our level we had no idea of the exchanges between the UK and Indonesian governments, but the outcome was that the VICTORIOUS Task Group was to transit the straits.

15 September was a busy day and my log book shows a sortie to deliver Operation Orders to the ships of the Task Group and the delivery of live headed torpedoes to certain ships. Because of the narrowness of the straits we were unlikely to be able to launch fixed wing aircraft during the transit. One of the major units of the Indonesian Navy was a former Russian Sverdlov cruiser, the *Irian*. One of our Observers, Lieutenant Nigel Fraser, noting that our Wessex HAS 1 weapon carriers could carry the 1000lb bombs used by the Buccaneers, came up with the idea that should we not have fixed wing cover a Wessex could mount an attack. The Sverdlov guns could not fire vertically so it would be a matter of dropping from overhead. Nigel designed a bombsight made out of loo rolls and we carried out trials using sacks of potatoes as bombs. Luckily at some point during the trial period someone pointed out that although the Wessex would be safe above the Sverdlov it certainly would not be during a quite slow and low approach. The trial was brought to a halt!

In the morning as we approached the straits we closed up at Action Stations. In the event we transited with no problems. We did meet an Indonesian frigate and a submarine and Indonesian and UK units exchanged identities and greetings. The UK had trained a lot of Indonesian naval personnel in the past and I suspect there were people we knew on those Indonesian units.

My last sortie with 814 was firstly simulating a fast patrol boat attack on VICTORIOUS, followed by an HF trial, followed by an anti-submarine screening exercise, and ending in acting as planeguard for a fixed wing launch and recovery. My 'flimsy' from 814 Squadron starts off by describing me as 'An efficient Anti-Submarine Observer', one up from ' average'!

I left 814 Squadron and HMS VICTORIOUS at the end of September 1964 heading for colder climes in Northern Ireland with 819 Squadron at RAF Ballykelly.

Chapter 6

RAF BALLYKELLY

819 Squadron/Wessex HAS 1.
November 1964 – March 1965

It is December 1964. It is a cold day in Northern Ireland at RAF Ballykelly and an 819 Wessex is being pulled out of the hangar ready to start the day's flying.

As Squadron Duty Officer I am overseeing preparations for the briefing and keeping an eye on the aircraft preparations. Suddenly a small commotion out on the line, something obviously not going to plan and I speed outside. Wessex 20 looks OK on one side but coming around the tail I see that one of the rotor blades has snapped in two. I'm sure that's not right!!

Whilst spreading the rotor blades it is necessary to turn two of the blades over and they flex – but they are not designed to snap in two. A small crowd gathers! A small nervous crowd I might say. 819 Squadron was a lodger unit at RAF Ballykelly the home to RAF Shackleton squadrons. It had been a wartime airfield and the RAF Squadrons were housed in what can only be described as Nissan huts with very basic toilet facilities. When it was decided to base 819 Squadron on the airfield a new brick building was erected equipped with flushing loo's. During the working day we would see a number of light blue visitors coming to avail themselves of the facilities. As can be imagined the stream grew during the day. Rotor blades are definitely not meant to snap in two.

To understand how this happened it is necessary to go back a month in time to November when 819 Squadron had detached three aircraft to HMS LOFOTEN. Lofoten was a former Landing Ship Tank converted to a helicopter training ship at Devonport Dockyard by welding the bow doors shut and fitting aviation fuel tanks on the tank deck. There was a shortage of flight decks for practising deck landings which was not overcome until RFA ENGADINE arrived in 1967. Lofoten was the interim solution, but, being flat bottomed was not designed to operate with embarked helicopters in the Atlantic during winter.

The 819 Squadron aircraft detachments had spent two periods at sea during November and due to the weather had achieved little flying. Consequently the aircraft had spent the majority of their sea time lashed down on the deck. HMS Lofoten had no hangar facilities and the aircraft were exposed to the weather. Ship movement caused the rotor blades to flex. These rotor blades consisted of an aluminium spar with pockets of glass fibre sheet bonded to the spar with a honeycomb structure in each pocket. In flexing, some of the bonding had weakened which allowed sea air and water into the rotor blade structure. Sea air/water and aluminium do not go well together and this combination ate away at the aluminium spar to the extent that when the blade was rotated in the blade spreading procedure it snapped.

On that December day we had no idea of how this had come about and there were some long reflective silences in both the engineer and aircrew crew-rooms.

All Wessex flying was ceased whilst the rotor blade was taken back to Westlands for examination.

Flying was resumed, as on 28 December as the Duty SAR crew, Lieutenant Commander Pete Burton the CO, and I flew to Rathlin Island to collect a man who was seriously ill requiring urgent medical treatment. Rathlin Island is the only inhabited Northern Ireland island located off the County Antrim coast. The gentleman was of generous proportions and it was only with difficulty we got him in the aircraft. He was known locally as 'the King of Rathlin

819 Squadron Wessex HAS Mk 1 with the 'hunted' in the Clyde. 1964

Ministry of Defence Crown Copyright 1964

819 Squadron Wessex HAS Mk 1 with broken blade. 1964

Ministry of Defence Crown Copyright 1964

819 Squadron Wessex HAS Mk 1 operating from HMS Lofoten. Note lack of hangarage. 1964

Ministry of Defence Crown Copyright 1964

Island'. We flew him to Ballymoney Hospital over a very snowy landscape.

In January 1965 three 819 Squadron Wessex HAS 1 were detached to ARK ROYAL to assist with her Work Up off the East Coast of Scotland.

On 28 February in the Moray Firth, when ARK ROYAL's Whirlwind 9 plane-guard helicopter went unserviceable, I was in an 819 Squadron Wessex, completing a running turn-round on deck - prior to a Screening sortie. We were tasked to take over the plane-guard duty for the next fixed wing launch and recovery.

It began snowing as the rescue diver clambered aboard with all his equipment. ARK ROYAL turned into the wind and by the time we reached the plane-guard station some 150 yards off the port quarter we were flying in thick snow. The aircraft was some

The author back on 'dry land' HMS Ark Royal. February 1965.

Ministry of Defence Crown Copyright 1965

75 feet above the sea with the main cabin door shut. I was in my seat on the port side of the cabin, Leading Seaman Humpleby the aircrewman and Naval Airman Pinnington the SAR diver were beside the closed main door, wearing despatcher harnesses waiting for the launch to begin.

Without warning the engine stopped (intake packed with snow as we later learnt), and we plummeted into the water, with no time for a MAYDAY to be transmitted. The aircraft rolled to starboard.

The Wessex had recently been fitted with two escape windows on the port side replacing the one small window. As the main door had been closed and the aircraft rolled to starboard I was virtually dry as I exited the forward port escape window. I found myself standing on the stringer between the two escape windows looking back into the aircraft to see where the aircrewman and diver were.

I was quite surprised to see the aircrewman and diver tussling over the main door. The diver wanted it open so he could exit through the door using his breathing apparatus. The aircrewman wanted it shut so that he had time to exit safely through the port side windows.

Thinking that I could assist the aircrewman, who by now was six feet below me, by giving him a hand up, I took a step backwards forgetting that there was a second escape window behind me. Big mistake, as I ended up back inside the aircraft, which was now half full of water. The aircrewman and I ended up exiting by our respective windows from the now half submerged Wessex, sliding, not too gracefully, into the water, inflating our dinghies and taking stock. The pilot, Lieutenant Tom Bowler, had long exited and was sitting in his dinghy. The diver having opened the main door and used his breathing apparatus to his advantage and appeared like a fish from under the water. So here we were in a fairly rough Moray Firth, bobbing around in a snow-storm, all safe and well.

ARK ROYAL had disappeared and it was later that we learnt about the events onboard. Amazingly the only witness to our ditching was a Midshipman who was on the quarterdeck. He had the good sense to ring the Bridge and tell them what he had seen. ARK ROYAL had cancelled the launch/recovery on entering the snow-storm and now started to circle back to where we had gone in.

In our dinghies we were all tied together and I had activated my SARBE. We were confident that ARK ROYAL would find us but the visibility was not great and the same snow storm was still raging.

Slowly, out of the gloom came ARK ROYAL, and began lowering a sea-boat. Also through the gloom appeared the 819 Squadron Wessex which had been on a screening exercise ahead of ARK.

Thankfully by now the snow-storm was easing as there was a likelihood that the second Wessex would suffer our fate. By the time the Wessex was in a position to lift us the snow-storm had passed. Tom Bowler, the aircrewman and myself were all winched up and returned to ARK ROYAL. The diver decided that his best bet was ARK ROYAL's sea boat!

Although I had had no contact with anyone when I activated the SARBE I wrote to Burndept Ltd, the makers of the SARBE equipment to say thank you. I was delighted some months later to be presented with a pewter 'SARBE tankard' by Burndept. I believe this was the first 'SARBE' tankard. All aircrew subsequently using their SARBE in anger received a similar tankard. My application to join the Goldfish Club was posted.

The Wessex HAS 1 (XM931) was recovered by HMMV Moorsman. On hitting the water the tailcone had been severed by the main rotor blades. The airframe was sold for scrap.

During my time on ARK ROYAL my parents had been involved in a serious car accident. Although their injuries were not life threatening they were serious. Following the ditching I felt events were running outside of my control and asked that I be taken off flying for some time. It was decided that I should be referred to the Admiralty Interview Board (AIB) at Seafield Park to decide my future.

I attended the AIB at Seafield Park and following two interviews it was decided I should be taken off flying for a period before returning to flying duties. I was to join HMS Grafton, a Type 14 frigate, in the 20th Frigate Squadron based in Londonderry. As we were living in a Married Quarter at Campsie just outside Londonderry this, on the face of it, appeared a good decision.

What neither Fiona, my wife, nor I knew at the time was that GRAFTON would only spend one weekend in Londonderry during my time onboard, the remainder of the time was spent in distant Home Waters and the Mediterranean!

Chapter 7

HMS GRAFTON

Type 14 Frigate. May – December 1965

I cannot recall my time on GRAFTON being a highlight of my naval career. The ship lacked a certain something. Although the Ships Company were individually very likeable people I cannot say we all pulled together. I was made the Communications Officer and also Special Sea Duty Officer of the Watch which meant I was the Officer of the Watch for certain evolutions such as entering/leaving harbour, going alongside, anchoring, close quarter manoeuvring, etc. And of course, as a Bridge Watchkeeper.

I joined GRAFTON in Portsmouth on 13 May and my first few weeks were spent listening and learning. The Captain was a hard taskmaster. At the end of my time onboard he tested me for my Watchkeeping Ticket. He failed me for answering one question on lights incorrectly. However he had trusted me as Officer of the Watch in all situations and I felt somewhat deflated not being awarded my Ticket.

In August 1965 GRAFTON was part of the Clyde Fleet Review which was reviewed by the Queen from HMY Britannia. The event seems to have been blanked from my memory as I have no recollections from the Clyde other than the Captain, in company with all other COs, going off for tea with the Queen on HMS CENTAUR.

GRAFTON's role was as an anti-submarine frigate and we carried out many anti-submarine exercises. During these exercises the method of communicating with the submarine was by throwing grenades into the sea. For example two grenades (explosions) would mean COMEX, start of exercise. The grenades would be thrown by the Officer of the Watch from the side of the bridge. Grenades had a ten second fuse. My cabin was just below the waterline on the port side just below the bridge wing. By delaying releasing the grenade after taking out the pin and dropping it straight down the ships side, it was discovered by one of my compatriots that I would be hurled from my bunk by the force of the explosion! I was unable to retaliate as his cabin was inboard. Happy times!

Following a series of exercises in the South West Approaches GRAFTON was scheduled to visit Douglas in the Isle of Man which would have meant anchoring off the town and running a boat routine into the small harbour. The weather forecast for the period of visit was not favourable for anchoring and running boats. A decision was made to go alongside in Peel Harbour which was on the western side of the Isle of Man. It was quite a tight approach to Peel but GRAFTON arrived alongside safely.

I had picked up the task of Duty Officer on the first night after a fairly long period at sea so I knew it would be quiet onboard, but probably not ashore! The Mayor of Douglas had invited the officers to a civic reception in Douglas that evening and transport was arranged to get them to the venue in Douglas some 13 miles away. We had shore power, so the boiler room was shut down for some minor maintenance.

At around 1900 the Peel Harbourmaster arrived onboard and informed me there was a phone call from Plymouth in his harbour office for the Duty Officer. I toddled down the harbour wall to take the phone call. It was the Flag Officer Plymouth Duty Staff Officer from the Plymouth Operations Room. The one-sided conversation went as follows; 'There has been a MAYDAY call from a merchant ship off the western coast of the Isle of Man in 'such and such' an approximate position. Are you ready to go to sea, if not, let me know immediately when you are'. Aye, Aye, Sir was my response.

HMS Grafton. 1954

Ministry of Defence Crown Copyright 1954

Back onboard I assembled the duty personnel, briefed them on the situation and gave the order to get ready for sea. First problem – the duty ERA, (Engine Room Artificer) had only joined that afternoon and it was his task to get the Boiler Room back up to steam. Not being that familiar with the routine would probably result in it taking longer than usual. At the time that seemed unimportant but I was to find out how important it was later.

Next task was to recall the ship's company from Douglas. I used the Harbour Masters office to talk to the Isle of Man police and they undertook to locate the officers who were hopefully in the Mayor's Parlour, and to get one of their patrol cars to go around the streets of Douglas requesting the GRAFTON ships company to return to their ship immediately.

Meanwhile I was casting an anxious eye down into the Boiler Room where there appeared to be clouds of steam coming from every corner and the Duty ERA was assuring me it would be alright 'in a minute'.

Eventually he assured me he had everything under control and was ready to go to sea.

By now it was around 2030, help was not coming over the horizon and I legged it down the harbour wall to phone the Plymouth Duty Staff Officer. I explained, we were ready for sea; I was a Lieutenant under training who had not yet got his watch-keeping ticket; the Captain had not yet returned, neither had any officers, although a small number of the ships company were back onboard. The question was, 'Do you have a plan to leave the jetty and get to sea?' the response, 'Yes, Sir'. 'Then go, as further communication from the merchantman had indicated they were taking to the life rafts'.

With my heart in my mouth I ran back down the jetty, up the gangway, up onto the bridge and took a microphone in my hand to broadcast to the ships company. Everyone had played their part and we were within seconds of casting off. Around the end of the harbour wall came a taxi literally flying down the harbour wall. Out stepped the Captain and the Navigator the two people that really mattered to me at that moment. The delay caused by the new Duty ERA had worked in my favour.

With a short delay whilst the Navigator worked out a safe way to exit the harbour wall we left Peel harbour.

For the next eight hours we searched the Irish Sea adjacent to the western side of the Isle of Man, in company with other shipping which was passing through the area. We found nothing. In the early hours of the morning we were ordered by Flag Officer Plymouth to give up the search and return to Peel. By this time most people onboard had been up all night and were quite downcast that there was nothing to show for our efforts. Had the merchant ship gone down and we had failed to locate any of the crew in their lifeboat(s)?

At about 0700 we approached Peel Harbour and started the slow turn to starboard to get around the end of the harbour wall and avoid the shallows on the port side. GRAFTON had a large single screw equipped with an Agouti system which dispensed air from the leading edges. This reduced the acoustic signature of GRAFTON particularly at low revolutions which meant we were less likely to be detected by any listening submarines.

As we turned in GRAFTON executed what can only be described as two marching paces to port as the screw bit into the mud. With the screw stopped we gently slid alongside the harbour wall and tied up. Within minutes the harbour wall was full of tired looking members of the ships company who had all been very well looked after by the good citizens of Peel.

Weeks later we were informed that the MAYDAY call had been a hoax. It had been perpetrated by a gentleman who had installed a maritime radio in his car and took delight in going to headlands, normally on the Lancashire coast and making hoax calls. He had been caught and was to be prosecuted. The Captain was court-martialled for running GRAFTON aground.

GRAFTON had finished her latest anti-submarine exercises in the Clyde. Our next stop was Chatham where we had to arrive on time in order to get into the Chatham Lock system. The weather forecast en-route was not good and we pounded on down through the Irish Sea in a Force 9 westerly gale. As we rounded The Lizard and started up the Channel the winds eased but the seas (the rollers) coming up our stern were massive. GRAFTON had only one screw (propeller), and because of the torque applied by that screw, in order to keep a straight course it was necessary for the Quartermaster (helmsman) to keep about two degrees of port rudder on. At 2000, just after passing Lizard Point, Alan Bannister, a recently joined Lieutenant took over as Officer of the Watch from me and I went down to have a shower and change prior to dinner. GRAFTON was now running before the easing storm with massive seas coming from astern such that the ship was aquaplaning down the waves and we still had to maintain our speed in order to make Chatham on time. The Captain appeared on the Bridge and suggested that as part of his training Alan should take the helm from the Quarter Master. Alan disappeared to the Quarter Masters position in a compartment aft of the Bridge. All of a sudden instead of standing in front of the hand basin I found myself lying/standing on the scuttle (porthole) on the side of the ship and GRAFTON appeared to be heading sideways. Alan had not applied the 2 degree port wheel and GRAFTON had 'broached to'. As GRAFTON had been sliding down a wave the stern had turned, the wave top had knocked GRAFTON sideways and we were now lying on our side in the trough of a wave with the next top of a wave coming down on to us. Luckily we had turned over to the starboard side which meant that the oncoming wave was not descending on the ships superstructure but onto the hull. Slowly, ever so slowly, GRAFTON returned to an upright position and down below I examined my cuts and bruises. Minutes later we were back on course and the ships company were counting cost of that one roll. Damage tended to be superficial but it was estimated that the cost to replace and repair was £10,000.

One of our Able Seaman (AB) was a gentle giant from Liverpool. Many a night watch was spent talking to him on the Bridge wing and he was a typical Scouser. He had gone AWOL (Absent Without Leave) prior to our visit to Chatham for the short refit. After a couple of weeks away from the ship he decided to return, with the aim of being discharged from the service. He stood outside a police station in Liverpool for a couple of days thinking he would be recognised as a deserter and arrested. No one recognised him and he marched into the police station and gave himself up. A few days later he arrived in Chatham under escort and the disciplinary proceedings started. There were only two officers left onboard, myself and Peter Jones, and as I was senior to Peter, he took over the role of Divisional Officer (looking after the Able Seaman's rights), and I heard the case as the Prosecuting Officer. All I could do was pass the case on to higher authority. The higher authority was the Captain in HMS PEMBROKE, the Chatham shore base. The AB was found guilty of desertion and sentenced to 60 days in Detention Quarters and a return to the service. In order to deter others from following in his footsteps the crime and the punishment are relayed to the ships company in a formal ceremony where the Punishment Warrant is read out to the offender and the ships company. Normally the Captain would read out the Warrant, but as he was on leave and I was the most senior officer left, it was up to me to read the Warrant. All was set, the ships company were assembled on the Iron Deck and the Master at Arms was taking charge of the ceremony. The offender arrived from the cells in HMS PEMBROKE. I began reading the Warrant with the Master at Arms to one side of me and the offender about ten paces in front of me flanked by two Naval Police. I got to the part in the Warrant where I read out the punishment, when as I finished, all turned to chaos. The AB kicked off big time. He had expected to be 'Discharged the Service' - instead he was to be retained and serve 60 days in DQs. From eyewitness accounts the Master at Arms shouted at me to run as the AB made in my direction; the two Naval Police tried to hang onto him but failed, the Master at Arms stepped in front of him and got bowled over, by which time I was on the other side of a metal door. He was restrained by a number of his shipmates and taken off to DQs. The importance of my getting out of the way is that had he managed to assault me he would have been up on more serious charges which could lead to prison. Everyone involved was well aware of this.

At an early point in my time on GRAFTON we had failed our harbour inspection carried out by Captain 20th Frigate Squadron. Another inspection date was arranged which coincided with our visit to Malta in late summer. I cannot remember the reason for the initial failure but one of Captain F's particular peccadillos was a well-presented ship by way of cleanliness, husbandry and painting. We had two days in Malta alongside before the inspection and plans were laid for painting. The voyage from the UK had involved a fair bit of sea time so there was going to be a lot of painting to catch up with. Day One in Malta saw the heavens open for twenty four hours, not a chance of getting any exterior painting done. Day Two, it stopped raining after lunch. The decision was made. No time to paint the entire ship so we would paint the half facing the jetty. I don't think anyone said 'he won't notice the rest' but that was the hope. Perhaps I should mention at this point that in July, his ship HMS Yarmouth, had failed it's sea inspection following a collision with HM S/M TIPTOE during an anti-submarine exercise. It had made for a good damage control exercise!

It was with some trepidation that Captain F and his staff were welcomed aboard on Day 3 in Malta. Would there be a backlash from their own inspection failure, or would they be understanding? Exactly half the ship looked immaculate, the other half looked like it had just returned from the Icelandic Wars!

Happily all parts of the inspection were passed, the half painted ship was explained and accepted without comment.

In November 1965 I was informed that I was to return to flying, joining 829 Squadron at HMS OSPREY at Portland in January. It was with some relief we packed up the Married Quarter at Campsie and moved to Portland.

Chapter 8

RNAS PORTLAND – HMS OSPREY

829 Squadron (Whirlwind HAS 7/Wasp HAS 1). January 1966 – June 1967

---

829 Squadron parented all the Wasp Flights which operated from frigates, and provided Whirlwinds for anti-submarine work-up exercises for ships coming through Flag Officer Sea Training (FOST) at Portland Naval Base.

For my next 18 months there was a lot of routine flying on Anti-Submarine exercises with ships working up under FOST in the Portland area. Trips to Battersea Heliport in London to deliver VIPs, and sorties to the Channel Islands and Caen in Northern France provided variety. The no-notice annual SMASHEX, simulating a submarine emergency, always raised one's pulse.

I was made the Squadron Operations Officer which included looking after the many Wasp Flights deploying world-wide. My major achievement was initiating a Helicopter Landing Site guide. Wasp Flights were landing at out of the way places all around the world. I requested all Flights to report back to me the necessary information that would assist the next Flight to land there, on a set proforma. I then collated that information for use Fleet-wide. This became the 829 Squadron Helicopter Landing Site Guide; the predecessor to the official RAF publication of today.

Life was enlivened by having to carry out the duties of Air Officer of the Day on the Air Station. This involved taking charge of Air Station matters when everything had closed down for the day. Doing security rounds of an airfield in the middle of the night with the rain lashing down has never been my idea of fun!

829 Squadron provided aircraft to ships coming out of refit for radar trials etc. Lieutenant Brian Ingledew was detached to RAF WEST MALLING, an airfield close to Chatham Dockyard, to act as a radar trials aircraft for a ship coming out of refit. Whirlwinds started their engine with the assistance of a starter cartridge. Whether Brian had used up his starter cartridges or had forgotten to take any, I cannot remember. But I do remember that Brian phoned through to the 829 Squadron Air Engineering Officer (AEO), Lt Mike Tothill, and left him the following message – 'Do not have any starter cartridges and am unable to start. One of the RAF maintainers has proposed wrapping a length of rope around the head, attaching a 3 tonner to the end of the rope which on moving away will spin up the rotor and start the engine'. Brian had a very dry sense of humour and Mike did not. There was a frantic phone call from Portland to West Malling that afternoon.

I left 829 Squadron in a hurry. It was 1 June, 1967, lunchtime, and I was sitting in the crewroom when the CO, Lt Cdr John Shrives comes in, offers his hand, and says, 'Goodbye Jim'. His message was I had to be in Gibraltar to join 848 Squadron (Wessex HU5) embarked on HMS ALBION, that evening. Arrangements were being made to get our Whirlwind with VHF out of deep maintenance as it was the only aircraft with the communications fit able to fly into the Westland Heliport at Battersea. Meanwhile, Lieutenant Dave Pink volunteered to drive me home to the other side of Weymouth to collect my gear. On arrival Fiona was surprised to see me, I quickly explained and as Dave came up to our front door Fiona slammed the door shut in his face (not deliberately). I packed without knowing where I was going. Threw in some 'whites' and essentials, kissed Fiona, and left. Brian Ingledew flew me to Battersea. We took off with maintainers still attaching panels and bits of equipment to the aircraft. One and a half hours later landed at Battersea to be met by my Appointer (Career Manager). We sped through London to Heathrow in his car and at

Heathrow met up with five other people. I remember Peter Voute who that morning had been happily flying off HMS BULWARK in an exercise off the north of Scotland. He had been rushed to Heathrow without the benefit of a home visit! BEA Viscount from Heathrow to Gibraltar where we were met by transport which took us to HMS ALBION in the Gibraltar Dockyard. None of us had any idea where ALBION was bound. A meal, find my bunk, and sleep. We sailed the following morning.

There was large degree of tension between Israel and Egypt/Syria/Jordan in the Eastern Mediterranean. This would culminate in the Six Day War from 5 Jun to 10 Jun between Israel and Egypt/Jordan and Syria being fought and won by Israel. In the minds of many on Albion and certainly those who had joined as reinforcements, such as myself, the thought was that we may be going East from Gibraltar. What was not on the radar was a civil war in Nigeria. The southwestern provinces of Nigeria were edging towards a secession from Nigeria to form the Republic of Biafra. The UK Government was watching events and was worried that should a civil war break out UK citizens would be threatened. On sailing on 2 June we turned south towards Nigeria. Eventually we were briefed as to where we were going at such a high speed. So fast that we would not have any support ships for some days after our arrival in the Gulf of Guinea. ALBION was to avoid all shipping so that our destination could not be deduced and we would remain undetected in the Gulf of Guinea. The Nigeria Civil War, or Biafran War, did start on 6 July 1967 and lasted until January 1970.

Although I had officially been sent to join 848 Squadron I was commandeered by ALBION to act as a communications link with our Embassy in Lagos. Most of my time was spent in a small office in the bowels of the ship deciphering and enciphering signals.

Back home the families and relatives of ALBION and 848 Squadron personnel were in the dark. Most would know ALBION had sailed on 2 June but no one knew where we had gone. No one onboard was allowed to send telegrams and our support RFA might have mail for us, but until it, or another unit, returned to Gibraltar or elsewhere with our outgoing mail there was no way of letting families know what was happening. I do remember that ALBION was able to receive telegrams. One officer had a very volatile South American wife and he had just disappeared without saying goodbye. She sent a series of telegrams threatening him with all sorts of dire consequences if he did not get in contact - which he put up on the Wardroom noticeboard!

I believe we spent six weeks in this covert role in the Gulf of Guinea as my logbook shows I did not fly with 848 Squadron until 19 Jul on a PINEX (navigation exercise) from RNAS Culdrose.

Chapter 9

HMS ALBION

848 Squadron/Wessex HU 5.
July 1967 - August 1968

Having returned from the Gulf of Guinea, disembarked from ALBION to Royal Naval Air Station (RNAS) Culdrose, (HMS SEAHAWK), I was now officially appointed to 848 Squadron as the Operations Officer.

Culdrose is located close to the town of Helston on the Lizard in Cornwall. At this time it was the home base of all Front Line Anti-Submarine and Commando Squadrons plus the helicopter pilot training squadrons. For many years it had more daily aircraft movements than Heathrow making it the busiest airfield in UK.

It was late on 22 August 1967 and I was preparing to leave the squadron building when the Culdrose Operations Room rang to say that 848 had been selected from 'a long list of one' to collect a VIP from the Scillies at 0900 tomorrow. With pilots disappearing quickly I eventually was able to persuade Lieutenant Mike Holcroft that he and I could do the sortie. At 0815 the following morning we lifted from Culdrose to fly to St Mary's Airport on the Scilly Islands. Our VIP was Harold Wilson, the Prime Minister, who had been recalled to London to deal with whatever the emergency was. It was either Southern Rhodesia and UDI or yet another financial crisis. Harold Wilson, his wife Mary and the Isles of Scilly police constable were there waiting for us at the grass strip. Mike remained 'burning and turning' whilst I dressed the Prime Minister in his safety equipment. I was very conscious that some months before the Prime Minister had been photographed in a Fleet Air Arm helicopter with his flying helmet on back to front which turned out to be front page news! Suitably equipped I made sure the Prime Minster was safely strapped in and indicated to Mary Wilson and the constable to retire from their position just outside the rotors. They waved back in return and appeared to move away. As Mike took off my final view was of Mary Wilson being forcibly pushed away by the downdraught, followed by a burly constable trying to prevent her from falling to the ground. We landed at Culdrose to transfer the Prime Minister to a fixed wing aircraft. He left without a thank you or a backward look. Maybe he remembered the flying helmet incident or he had seen Mary flying across the airfield without wings!

In early September 1967 following a short work-up the squadron embarked in ALBION and headed south. I flew into Hastings Airfield in Sierra Leone to collect mail on 19 September, and into Port Reitz Airfield (Mombasa) in Kenya for mail on 8 October.

During our passage up the East Coast of Africa we made a five day stop in Durban. At the ship's cocktail party I was able to 'baron strangle'. 'Baron strangling' is very much a naval occupation and consists of meeting and cultivating a 'local' normally at a cocktail party, and then getting invited 'up homers' which is to come and stay the night or enjoy the hospitality of that person. 'Baron strangling' can literally be accepting a drink in a bar to being invited to a weekend at their home. It is never meant to be a one way process and the 'baron' is always invited for a tour of the ship, a lunch onboard or to have his/her hospitality repaid in some way. At the cocktail party I met up with the British Consul and his wife and was invited to come and spend a couple of nights at their house and the wife would show me around the Durban markets. I left the ship with an overnight bag omitting to tell anyone where I was going. Two days later I returned to Albion to find that one of our squadron ratings had been killed following a fall from a high rise building in the city. The squadron had 'cleared lower

HMS Albion Replenishing At Sea (RAS). Note chutes down into hangar for potato sacks and other dry provisions. 1967

Ministry of Defence Crown Copyright 1967

deck' - that is all squadron personnel had been called together for a briefing and short service. I had been missing. Following a one sided interview with the CO my punishment was to be part of the potato party on the next Replenishment At Sea (RAS). This party was responsible for the handling of the potato sacks coming across from the stores ship and was all manual labour. I deserved it.

Coming into Durban, ALBION had witnessed a little bit of history. From April 1940 to August 1945 Mrs Perla Siedle Gibson, the Lady in White, had sung to troopships which were on their way to battlefields in the Middle and Far East whilst standing on the end of the northern breakwater. As a young woman Perla had trained as a soprano in Germany. She sang traditional songs such as 'There'll always be an England' and Land of Hope and Glory.

Amazingly, The Lady in White sang us in. For our leaving Durban it was somewhat different. Perla was invited to sing us out from the flight-deck and once we had cleared the harbour the squadron Wasp piloted by Lt Dave Tink flew her back into Durban. Perla passed away in 1971 just before her 83rd birthday. In 1995 a statute was unveiled by her two surviving children close to the Durban Ocean Terminal.

HMS ALBION was tasked with supporting the British Withdrawal from the Aden Protectorate in October/November 1967. As during the withdrawal ALBION would be providing support and air cover it was thought sensible to have a Naval Liaison Officer assisting within the RAF Khormaksar Operations Room. As the Squadron Operations Officer I was selected for the task.

On 12 October 1967 I was flown into RAF Khormaksar and began watch-keeping in the RAF Ops Room. Primarily my task was to coordinate RN helicopter operations with RAF and Army operations as the military perimeter shrank in towards RAF Khormaksar. There was a lot going on and I found myself very much embedded into the RAF watchkeeping system dealing with all UK Naval Task Force matters; from tasking 848 Squadron aircraft; coordinating the movements of civilian trooping flights arriving from the UK to take personnel back to UK; travel arrangements being made for members of FLOSY (Front for the Liberation of Occupied South Yemen) and the NLF (National Liberation Front) who were fighting both between themselves, and with us, to take over Aden once withdrawal was complete. There were often some tricky negotiations dealing with the latter. It soon became obvious that I could not be available 24 hours a day and I requested assistance from ALBION. It arrived in the form of Sub Lieutenant Dixie Dean, one of the 848 Squadron pilots.

Daily life was not easy. The RAF Khormaksar perimeter was shrinking and we were moving almost daily from Married Quarter to Married Quarter to remain within the perimeter. Life was not normal and relaxation was difficult but working in the Operations Room had its compensations. The civilian trooping flights could initially refuel at RAF Khormaksar with the aim of running down the stocks as much as possible so there would be little left on withdrawal day. Whilst the flights were refuelling at Khormaksar the crews made a nightstop. It was down to us in the Operations Room to ensure the crew had accommodation and food. Strangely enough the accommodation for the male crew members was always in a different Married Quarter block to those of the female crew. All were given the warning not to leave their block until they were collected the following morning. Equally strangely the female crew members were always accommodated in the block that was occupied by the Operations Room staff! Yes, there were some very memorable parties and there were occasions when an 848 Squadron Wessex mysteriously went U/S (unserviceable – unable to return to Albion that night!). and the crew had to nightstop on the airfield on the same evening as a trooping flight arrived.

One incident remains in my mind from a party. Everyone in the block had gathered in the second floor Married Quarter. It was quite late in the evening and we were celebrating having to move from this block to another one the following day. All sorts of silliness was going on and one thing that had caught on was sliding down the fire escape rope from the second floor balcony, running in through the front door and running up the stairs to rejoin the party. The fire escape rope was coiled up on the balcony. After a few beers or two a senior officer from the RAF Regiment decided it was his turn to do the course. He grabbed the escape rope and leapt over the balcony only to find he had grabbed the wrong end. There was a dull thud and a cry. Looking down from the balcony all we could see was a figure spread eagled on the sand. Down the stairs at speed to the sight of him walking in through the front door. A combination of the amount of drink, the way he hit the ground and the soft sand meant he had broken both legs and both arms – but was otherwise OK!! He refused to be casevac'd back to the UK and spent the remainder of the withdrawal period in plaster.

The British Government had been told by FLOSY and the NLF that it was to leave all the equipment in place and not to take any out to the Task Force off Aden. Dixie and I were tasked to get as many vehicles to the UK Embassy at Steamer Point from where they could be lifted by helicopter out to the Task Force under cover of darkness. The vehicles in question were mainly Minis, senior officer's cars, and Land Rovers.

The route from RAF Khormaksar to Steamer Point had to go down Ma'alla Straight, there was no other option. Ma'alla Straight was about a mile long with high buildings on either side set well back from the actual road. There had been incidents where local terrorist groups (FLOSY/NLF and others) had strung piano wire or suchlike across the road designed to catch a military vehicle at windscreen height. In the hot weather many Land Rovers would have the windscreen down with tragic consequences. Most military vehicles had a vertical metal pole mounted at a forward facing angle on the front bumper to combat this tactic. Unfortunately the ships Land Rover Dixie and I had been provided with did not have such a metal pole. Being young and foolish and obeying the last order – to get vehicles to Steamer Point, we decided that we could do the runs by driving our Land Rover whilst leaning sideways and driving looking forwards down the side of the vehicle. Traffic was minimal at dusk when we made most of the runs and putting the other vehicle as the lead on the way to Steamer Point reduced the risk. The return journey was always the more exciting.

During the last few days of the withdrawal date an 820 Squadron Wessex from HMS EAGLE made an emergency landing at RAF Khormaksar. It was adjudged not repairable within the available timescale. Without a heavy lift helicopter there was only one way to get the Wessex back to EAGLE – by a landing craft from HMS ALBION. This involved towing the Wessex from Khormaksar to a slipway outside the perimeter. The 820 Squadron Senior Pilot, Lt Cdr Ben Bathurst, accompanied the small armed convoy that made its way to the slipway. Although on paper a Wessex would fit into an LCVP, the measurements had not allowed for various aerials protruding. There followed some discussions about removing aerials in accordance with maintenance manuals, or, removing them quickly. Taking into consideration the situation of falling tide and the approaching darkness, my priority of quick removal prevailed and a slightly more damaged, but repairable Wessex made its way back to EAGLE.

To boost our morale Dixie and I had been issued with Sterling machine guns and two magazines as our personal weapons. All went well until I discovered I had 'mislaid' one of the magazines. Through my work in the Ops Room I had established a good working relationship with Major Sparrow in the Parachute Regiment. I rang him to ask for advice. Within 15 minutes a paratrooper arrived in the Ops Room with a brown envelope. I returned my Sterling and magazines to the Armoury in the same condition as I received them.

HMS Albion mail cart. The morale booster. 1967
Ministry of Defence Crown Copyright 1967

848 Squadron Wessex HU Mk 5 over Ma'alla Straight Aden. 1967

Ministry of Defence Crown Copyright 1967

And so we came to the last day, the final withdrawal – 29 November 1967. Dixie and I had arranged to be picked up by one of our Squadron aircraft and the detail of how we selected the spot or the time to be picked up elude me now – some 53 years later. I remember the spot was close to a hangar and within sight of the main perimeter fence and that the pick-up time was 0930. At 0930 no sign of an aircraft, we could see helicopter activity with small groups being picked up on the rest of the airfield.

Behind the perimeter fence there was a sizable crowd of Adeni's gathering. The base was to be handed over to the South Arabian Army and we could see no sign of them. After one of the longest fifteen minutes in my life our very welcome transport arrived piloted by Lieutenant Ian Oak-Rhind and my records show we were picked up at 0945 for the ten minute flight back to ALBION. Task complete.

Over Christmas 67/68 the squadron disembarked to RNAS Sembawang on Singapore Island.

848 Squadron had a lot of very young pilots. From memory I think there were some 18 Sub Lieutenant pilots at one point in my time on the squadron. Navigation over the jungle was not a skill taught during flying training in the UK but for the next few months it was a requirement. Luckily I had the experience from my service in 814 Squadron to be able to teach the basics. In Malaysia there were quite adequate maps showing the main water courses which were crucial to jungle navigation. Without any other aids using Dead Reckoning (Speed v Distance) over dense flat jungle to anticipate arrival over the next water course becomes crucial. Due to dense foliage there may only be a few seconds in which to see the water. In Malaysia there was also normally a large hill/mountain somewhere on the horizon to take a bearing from as a confirmation that the aircraft was on the right track. Practice makes perfect and jungle navigation exercises were commonplace. The ability to find or re-find a site in the jungle, which will only be visible for a short duration due to the size and height of the surrounding jungle foliage was emphasised shortly after our arrival when a light aircraft went missing over the Malaysian jungle and we were requested to assist with the search.

The make-up of a Commando Squadron with 18 Wessex HU 5 was around 30 Pilots (RN, RM and Army Air Corps); including the Commanding Officer and Senior Pilot; 1 Observer, 25 Aircrewmen (Royal Marines as well as RN); an Air Engineering Officer (AEO) and Deputy, and over 150 Air Engineers and Supply personnel, (mainly Stewards/Chefs). There was also a Mobile Air Operations Team (MAOT) with an Air Traffic Control Officer, Sub Lieutenant Alex Crow, in charge. The MAOT were deployed with their Land Rover and Trailer to provide Air Traffic facilities which included laying out landing sites and crucially providing night landing aids at landing sites when night operations were required. Night vision goggles had not yet been invented. The MAOT also maintained communications with ALBION whilst ashore.

Lieutenant Commander Peter Williams was the Commanding Officer known as The Boss.

The squadron was tasked to take the Commander in Chief Far East forces, an RAF senior officer, from his residence in downtown Singapore out to HM submarine RORQUAL somewhere off the Malaysian coast on 5 January.

The Boss decided to do the sortie and asked me to go along and do the navigation.'Junglies', that is Wessex HU Mk 5 pilots, were always a bit wary flying out of sight of land and the Boss

Royal Naval Air Station Sembawang (HMS Simbang). Disembarked squadrons used the larger hangar to the right. Also served as barracks for a Royal Marine Commando. 1968

Ministry of Defence Crown Copyright 1968

thought I would ensure we didn't get lost! On the 4 January we did a recce of the CinCs residence and the landing site. We had a grid reference, so what could go wrong? Landing site looked a bit tight and there appeared to be some flower beds close by, but it was an official landing site, so we returned to Sembawang.

Next day at 0700 we lifted off from Sembawang and confidently flew south for a 0720 pick-up. We did a pass over the landing site and then ran in. Seemed a bit tighter than yesterday, but we descended from a high hover into what now appeared to be quite a formal garden. Strangely the main residence was totally shuttered and there was no sign of any party waiting to be picked up. A few flower pots were being lifted up by our downwash and the aircrewman, cautiously gave the Boss instructions.

We landed safely, although the garden did seem to be suffering. No sign of any movement from the house. The Boss asked the aircrewman to go across to the house and see if he could raise the occupants. As he left the aircraft the front door of the residence opened and a lady in a dressing gown and long flowing hair appeared gesticulating wildly, indicating in the direction in which we were pointing. Meanwhile more plants seemed to be deserting the garden. Aircrewman got back into the aircraft and suggested we might be in the wrong place!

We took off and rose about 50 feet; there ahead of us, not 150 yards away, was a landing site, with a windsock and a small party of two. With infinite caution we landed, embarked our passengers, and proceeded towards the RV with Rorqual. The remainder of the flight proceeded without incident.

During the flight back to Sembawang it was decided, as the Boss had a meeting onboard ALBION that morning, I would take the squadron 2CV and get down to the CinCs residence and apologise for our mistake in order to forestall anything worse.

An hour later I entered the residence gates. The garden was to put it mildly, a disaster area. There were few flowers remaining, but the main damage was to the flower pots, some huge and ceramic, and there were only a handful left. I plucked up my courage and went in through the front door. The CinCs lady was not there and I was received by the CinCs aide-de-camp who by trade was Army.

The aide-de-camp was highly amused by the whole thing and told me not to worry about anything. Over a cup of coffee he told me that the RAF had been asked to assess landing in front of the residence with a Whirlwind and had said it was impossible. For some reason he was highly chuffed they had been proved wrong.

We never heard anything more about this incident, but the state of that garden has remained with me.

Move on a few months. Because of a shortage of aircrew and therefore people doing long stints in the Far East, a mid-term leave system had been introduced.

The Boss, myself and four or five others were sent back to the UK for a fortnights leave. On arrival in the UK we had to phone the Appointer (Career Manager) and he would organize the return trooping flight to Singapore.

On the appointed day we all met up at RAF Lyneham for our return trooping flight. The party consisted of one Lieutenant Commander, three Lieutenants, one Sub Lieutenant and an Army Air Corps Captain on exchange with 848 Squadron, Captain David Ashley. We were informed that we would be trooping out to Singapore in a VIP Comet 4C which was going out to take the CINC Far East on a trip to Australia.

We were called forward as a group with, Captain Ashley first followed by the Boss etc. The first person to realise what was happening was the Boss who grabbed Dave Ashley's bag to carry on for him. We were ushered into the VIP seating area in the Comet and being looked after rather well. By now we had all twigged – the RAF had put us all together as an RN staff going out to Singapore headed by an RN Captain. The remainder of those on the flight were put in the 'definitely economy' seating at the rear of the Comet.

We enjoyed excellent food and even alcohol was served during the first leg to RAF Akrotiri in Cyprus. 'Captain' Ashley was informed that the CO of RAF Akrotiri would be looking after him whilst we were refueling. Dave was briefed as well as we could on how to maintain the façade whilst he was with the RAF CO. We landed, Dave was ushered off first, met by the RAF CO and disappeared. We stayed with the plebs in the Transit Lounge.

Next leg was to Bahrain, landing at about 0200 with a nightstop in the RAF Muharraq Transit Mess. The crew informed Dave that they had radioed ahead to the CO of HMS JUFAIR and he would be met and hosted in HMS JUFAIR. This was a problem. The CO would almost certainly check the Navy List and find out that Captain Ashley did not exist. We decided the best thing was for Dave to come totally clean, explain the situation, and hope the CO of JUFAIR would agree to let us continue.

We landed, Dave was ushered out first, the CO of JUFAIR met Dave at the bottom of the steps, listened to what he had to say, turned on his heel and walked away. We were rumbled.

After a short and uncomfortable night we were 'welcomed' back onto the Comet and put back with the plebs in the economy seats for the next leg to Gan and then onto Singapore. But at least half of the 23 hour flight had been in relative comfort.

And the connection with the first story? – Dave Ashley was a superb cartoonist and drew a cartoon of our January landing at the CinC's residence with flowers, leaves, flower pots all disappearing under the downdraft of a Wessex 5, – with an apology from the crew. The Comet crew were asked to see that the CinC received it – but have no way of knowing whether he did or not.

Peter Williams passed away in 2020, and when I hear his name mentioned I think about flower-pots and Comets.

The squadron spent quite a lot of time disembarked to RNAS Sembawang, an airfield with a very chequered history. It was built in 1937 for the RAF but by 1939 had passed to RN control; in 1940 to the Royal Australian Air Force; in 1942 to Japanese control. In December 1945 it became HMS SIMBANG and in December 1947 it went into Care and Maintenance (C&M). 1948 saw the airfield on loan to the RAF and in 1949 back to C&M. In 1950 back to RN control as HMS SIMBANG. Between 1957 and 1962 back into C&M. 1962 recommissioned as HMS SIMBANG as both a Naval Air Station and a Royal Marine Barracks, until 1971 when the complex was turned over to the Singapore Air Defense Command.

At Stand-Easy (break time) the 'Magnolia Man' would arrive on his bicycle with a refrigerated locker containing bottles of 'pink milk', always popular with aircrew and maintainers (other flavours were available!). Wherever we were in Malaysia a Magnolia Man would turn up. Their intelligence network was superb. Look closely at the foot of the tree in the accompanying photograph.

During February, March and April the Squadron was involved in exercises around Mersing, a grass airstrip on the East coast of Malaya. Late March/early April we established a Forward Operating Base (FOB) on the airstrip. 66 Squadron RAF with Belvederes was located to the south end of the strip with our Wessex 5s to the north. All were under canvas. The Army had provided 3 tonners to ourselves and the RAF to take up the essentials like tents, shovels for digging latrines, etc., from Singapore. On arrival at the site for our camp I received a message that our 2 x 3 tonners were in the Army camp some three miles from the airstrip. The only two people available to collect the 3 tonners were Peter Railton-Woodcock, the Deputy Squadron Air Engineering Officer and myself. A squadron Haflinger drove us to the Army base. A quite officious Army person indicated the RN 3 tonners and wanted to see our driving licences which entitled us a drive a 3 tonner. Neither Peter nor I, had ever driven a 3 tonner, let alone possessed a licence. We pointed out that we had not expected to be asked for our licences in the middle of the jungle and would he kindly let us get on our way so that we could start setting up our camp. With lots of grumbling and jobsworth noises he gave us the keys. The next few minutes were interesting. There were more levers and knobs than I was used to but having found where to insert the key and started the engine I tentatively let in the clutch and stalled. The officious Army person was standing watching this performance. Luckily, Peter had got his truck moving which shielded me from the Army person. A second start and clutch engagement was successful, I moved forward aiming to follow Peter. I cannot remember if I ever changed gear as the track was full of holes and bends and it

Mersing airfield, Malaysia. 848 Squadron encampment. 1968
Ministry of Defence Crown Copyright 1968

was with relief that I reached the airstrip which was at least flat, no holes and I didn't have to work hard to to keep the truck in a straight line. On arrival at the 'camp site' it was all hands to the pump to get our kit unloaded, tents up, latrines dug etc. But there was a problem, the contents of my 3 tonner were certainly not ours! They appeared to belong to the RAF with such items as the Mess 'Silver', packets of cereal and other 'luxury' items not normally found in ration packs. Obviously our brethren in light blue were intending to live well during the exercise. Various suggestions as to what to do with the 3 tonner were aired, lose it in the jungle, hold it to ransom. Sanity prevailed and it was driven to the other end of the grass airstrip and returned to its rightful owners. Meanwhile the Haflinger sped off to the Army camp with a real 3 tonner driver to find our missing truck.

Mersing airfield, Malaysia. Morning Colours. 1986
Ministry of Defence Crown Copyright 1968

Mersing airfield, Malaysia. Start of a new day. Note the 'Magnolia Man' under the tree. 1968

'Runs ashore' in Singapore were always interesting. There is no definition in the Royal Navy of a 'run ashore'. It could be to take afternoon tea in a local hotel, it could be a beer-swilling, rousing singing competition in a local pub. Anyone starting out or invited on a 'run ashore' had no idea how it would turn out. Having caught your 'fast black', which were local illegal taxis, normally large Mercedes saloons borrowed from relatives, and extremely cheap as they carried as many passengers as could be fitted in, the run ashore proceeded into Singapore city. Apart from the normal bars there were places like Change Alley to be visited. Change Alley was the first place you looked if you had any kit stolen from the base. Everything and anything was on sale. Bugis Street or Boogie Street as it was known in the 60s was the home of transvestites, trans people, kai-tai's, lady boys and prostitutes. All

Mersing airfield, Malaysia. Morning ablutions. 1968

were beautiful people and no one could tell who was what or who. To spend time sitting at a table drinking a cool beer and watching the antics of foreign visitors and the 'residents' of Bugis Street was an education. Around the corner in Albert Street was 'Alberts'. Alberts was a tatty looking restaurant with tables outside, inside and upstairs. All cooking was done in the street by the drains. The fare was delicious and to my memory no one ever suffered from food poisoning! One brave member during a meal there asked for Sheeps Brain Soup. A bowl of what looked like water with a sheep's brain floating in it duly arrived. Not for me. Runs ashore could end in two ways. Firstly with coffee in the Singapura Hotel in Orchard Road. Orchard road was a main thoroughfare with big shops and most nights a huge market which filled both sides of the road. The coffee shop was open all night and was always busy. Secondly, you could take a 'fast black' (taxi, almost certainly operating illegally), back to Nee Soon the little village just outside the main gate to Sembawang. There at Virgins Corner you could get an 'Egg Banjo' (Fried Egg in a roll or between bread slices) throughout the night to make up for the breakfast you were about to miss.

I bought an elderly MGTD from one of the Royal Marines at Sembawang. In the short time that I owned it driving around Singapore Island was fun. One evening driving down Orchard Road the car briefly lurched to one side, like a puncture. Two seconds later in the passenger seat appeared Bill Bailey, one of our young 2nd Lieutenant Royal Marine pilots. He had leapt from the window of a car driving alongside me into what passed as my backseat. On reflection he was lucky not to have killed himself. I sold the MG to an airline pilot who flew it to Hong Kong in a cargo plane. Over 50 years later I cannot remember how I afforded to buy the MG or why I bought it. It was fun whilst it lasted.

Come the summer of 1968, it was time to stop enjoying my job as the Squadron Operations Officer and move back to serious flying. I was appointed to 360 Joint RN/RAF Squadron at RAF Watton.

Chapter 10

RAF WATTON

360 Joint RN/RAF Squadron (Canberra T17)
12 August – 11 November 1968

R AF Watton is in Norfolk close to East Dereham. We lived in Yaxham in a 16th century three storey restored cottage in the grounds of a once grand house.

360 Squadron was tasked with providing Electronic Warfare facilities during exercises and acting as targets for Air Defence exercises. I would train as an EW operator first and then qualify as a Navigator. Aircrew were a mixture of RN and RAF personnel.

My time in 360 Squadron was to be short.

After a couple of flights I became aware that I was suffering from vertigo. This manifested itself as my brain telling my body that (for example) following the aircraft diving, the aircraft was continuing to dive and continuing down and under in a circle, although in reality it had pulled out and was straight and level. It was very uncomfortable, but I hoped I would be able to cope as time went on.

On 22 September, operating out of RAF Lossiemouth, my aircraft, piloted by Lieutenant 'Stumpy' Faulkner RN, headed north to take part in Exercise Silver Tower. The brief was to cover a raid by Buccaneers on a naval task force. The raid was delayed and we spent a lot of time loitering waiting for the Buccaneers to appear. We supported the delayed raid and headed south for Lossiemouth only to learn that Lossiemouth had been declared RED due to weather. A Har, basically a thick fog, had set in and recovery to the airfield was problematical as the cloud base was less than 200 feet and the visibility less than 800 metres. We therefore had to divert, probably to RAF Leuchars. It was at this point we discovered there was not sufficient fuel to get to a diversion airfield.

The RAF do not do 'back in the saddle' flying-; that is where a pilot might have been off flying for a period and needed to get their hand back in. (The Royal Navy does). Stumpy had been on three weeks leave in Italy, had not flown up to Lossiemouth and this was his first flight after a three week plus lay-off.

Stumpy decided our only option was to persuade Lossiemouth to take us in despite it being declared RED. Lossiemouth agreed. The Ground Controlled Approach (GCA) descent into Lossiemouth was not a good experience from the start when Stumpy said 'I'm not sure I can do this!' The commentary from the GCA Controller saying 'you are low on the glide slope' continually, plus the navigator, Flight Lieutenant Wedderburn tightly gripping his ejection seat pull handle between his knees, did not give me any confidence. The descent must have taken between 4 and 5 minutes, and my everlasting memory is Stumpy continually saying 'I can't do this'. Of course Stumpy did manage to get us on the ground safely and I am here to tell the tale.

I left the aircraft to meet the detachment Squadron Leader and my first words were 'you will not get me up in one of those again'. Without further ado I was on a train south that evening heading towards the Admiralty Interview Board (AIB) at Seafield Park. This meant I missed the inquiry into why we were short of fuel unable to divert!

The members of the AIB decided that I should immediately return to helicopter flying. This led to my next appointment as Staff Officer in 700(S) Intensive Flying Trials Squadron for the Sea King HAS Mk 1. However before joining 700(S) I had to complete

Canberra T17

Reproduced by kind permission of Kevin Slade.

a Wessex HAS Mk3 familiarisation with 706 Squadron at RNAS Culdrose as I had to get up to speed with the equipment in the Mk3 which would also be fitted in the Sea King.

We left Yaxham at midday to drive down to Helston in Cornwall to our newly allocated married quarter. All our belongings following on in a removal van. We had arranged to meet the removal van the following morning at the married quarter. We arrived at around 0800 to find the removal van crew had parked their van on the main road adjacent to our quarter, had thrown everything over a five foot Cornish hedge into our garden, and departed back to Norfolk. To say we were not amused is to put it mildly.

Chapter 11

RNAS CULDROSE

700(S) Squadron/Sea King HAS 1.
March 1969 – July 1970

The Sea King was preceded by the Wessex HAS Mk3. The RN had moved forward from the Whirlwind to the Wessex HAS Mk 1, from out of which the Mk 3 developed with an improved sonar (Type 195) and a Ekco radar (ARI 5995). These improvements reduced the endurance/payload performance of the Mk 3 compared to the Mk 1 and it was recognised that improvements in submarine performance needed improvements in anti-submarine helicopter technology. Reduction in endurance was in part overcome by Helicopter In Flight Refuelling or HIFR, where the screening Wessex 3 ahead of the force was able to refuel from a screening frigate obviating the need to return to the carrier. In the accompanying photograph a Wessex 3 is refuelling from HMS ROTHESAY, a Whitby Class frigate. Note the frigate's own Wasp is still operating.

In 1967 Westland Helicopters had obtained a licence to build a UK version of the US HSS-2. Fitting the Wessex HAS Mk 3 radar, sonar and Marconi Doppler Navigation system in the new aircraft would meet new requirements. The aircraft would be called the Sea King HAS 1 with uprated UK engines and a Mk31 Flight Control System by Louis Newmark. The FCS in the Mk 3 was a Duplex system (fail/safe), but had proved so reliable that the Sea King version was to return to Simplex. With 2 torpedoes carried the Sea King would still be able to complete a 4 hour sortie in temperate climates. The Sea King came with improved endurance and payload and was likened to the equivalent of a small frigate.

700(S) Squadron was to be the Intensive Flying Trials Unit for the Sea King HAS Mk 1. The aim of the squadron was to prove the aircraft was ready in all respects for service in the Fleet. This included flying and engineering procedures and as time went on to train aircrew and maintainers who would make up the first Front Line squadrons.

700(S) Squadron did not commission until 19 August and initially Lieutenant Commander Jim Flindell, the Senior Observer, and myself were appointed to do the groundwork for the squadron to be ready to begin the Intensive Flying Trials from that date.

Jim and I spent time preparing the squadron building - the necessary infrastructure such as coffee machines and fridges to sustain the aircrew! We attended manufacturers familiarisations around the country, learnt as much as we could about the new aircraft, and generally kept busy.

The Captain of Culdrose 'Slug' Notley, was very keen to hold a Youth Sunday at Culdrose involving all youth organisations from across Cornwall. His vision was a parade, a service, a judging of the turnout of the various contingents, and a presentation to the best unit. He looked around Culdrose for volunteers to organise his Youth Sunday. He identified two officers who apparently did not have a job as their unit had not yet commissioned, and 'invited' us to 'get organising'.

The story I have to tell is not about the Youth Sunday which went off very well, but an event leading up to the day.

Following some time researching a suitable VIP who could take the parade and judge the contingents, we asked Princess Chula Chakrabongse, who had a position in the British Red Cross and lived close to Bodmin. The Princess was the wife of the

Siamese racing driver Prince Chula Chakrabongse. Contact with the Princess confirmed she would be happy to attend the parade, judge the contingents and present the trophy. Sometime later Jim Flindell received a phone call from the Princess asking if it would be acceptable for her to wear her British Red Cross uniform as there was to be a Cornish Red Cross contingent present on the day. There were almost certainly other matters to discuss with the Captain and we booked in to see him.

'Slug' Notley was a very straightforward Naval Officer. For example, he had been the Commanding Officer of a frigate on a visit to Grimsby. The Mayor of Grimsby invited him and the officers to

737 Squadron Wessex HAS Mk 3 operating off Portland, Dorset. (1969)
Ministry of Defence Crown Copyright 1969

737 Squadron Wessex HAS Mk 3 Helicopter In Flight Refuelling (HIFR) with HMS Rothesay. Note: Wasp HAS Mk 1 taking off from Rothesay's Flight Deck. (1968)

Ministry of Defence Crown Copyright 1968

a Civic Reception in Grimsby Town Hall. A car was organised to take him to the reception. Five minutes after the car had been due to arrive a bin lorry stopped on the jetty, going about its business. 'Slug', fed up with waiting asked the crew of the bin lorry if they would take him to the Town Hall. 'Delighted', they said, and he arrived at the reception in the bin lorry in his best uniform with sword and medals. He would have hugely enjoyed that.

Jim and I arrived for our meeting, it was just coming to the end of a hot afternoon. We sorted out our queries, but when we raised the question of British Red Cross uniform or not, Slug was obviously slightly irritated and made some observations which today would be decidedly politically incorrect. Having discussed and agreed that uniform was acceptable Jim and I got up to go. I opened the door to see Slug's next visitors – 6 newly promoted young WRNS officers. As Jim came through the door after me Slug yelled out 'And tell her what knickers to wear' for the whole world to hear. The effect upon six young WRNS officers was electric, as though a switch had been thrown. A moment not to be forgotten.

I have already mentioned Jim and I attended manufacturers familiarisations in the run up to commissioning. One such event was in the Ekco factory at Chelmsford in Essex. The engineer tasked with giving us the familiarisation was commuting on a daily basis from Ely, some 100 miles away. In conversation with the engineer we expressed surprise at his daily commute. His response was a surprising one.

He had been living in Ilford in a long row of old terraced houses. His wife did not work and was in their house most of the day. His wife began saying that she felt uneasy during the day as she felt there were people in the house and there were smells she could not identify. To start with they laughed off this feeling. But his wife persisted to the extent that they searched the house from top to bottom and finding nothing thought to cut into the loft space. On cutting into the loft space they were able to see from one end of the terraced houses loft spaces to the other end. They had cut into a dormitory of camp beds and sleeping bags. The entire loft space was taken up by migrant workers coming in from one of the houses, entering the loft and using the space to live. They made the decision to move from the London area and Ely had fitted the bill. At the time Jim and I found this tale hard to believe, but I have now heard similar stories and that tale has remained with me for over 50 years.

August 1969 saw not only the 700(S) commissioning but also the birth of our son, John. The squadron had an American

Exchange Officer, Lieutenant Andy Granuzzo USN, due to join. I oversaw the arrangements for his Married Quarters which would not be available until after his arrival in Cornwall. I arranged for accommodation for him and his wife in a local hotel. The first weekend following his arrival Fiona and I invited Andy and Mary-Ellen for Sunday lunch. Over lunch we learnt that Mary-Ellen had been a nursing sister in the largest maternity hospital in New Orleans. Mid-afternoon and Fiona's waters broke, which was not a problem as it was to be a home birth. To our surprise Mary-Ellen insisted on leaving immediately. I thought she would have been a useful person to have around. They left, the midwife arrived and John's birth was without complications. I later learnt that Mary-Ellen left quickly as she was terrified that if something had gone wrong and she had been involved she would have been sued. Later Andy asked where he could purchase a revolver for personal security. Andy had noticed in a daily newspaper that there had been a murder in Newcastle! It took a bit pf persuading for him to understand that that had been the only murder in the UK that day. It had been usual for him to carry a weapon in his car in Florida as personal security. Both Andy and Mary-Ellen were lovely people and we had them and the next USN Exchange Officer, Jim O'Brian and his wife Beth for next door neighbours for a number of years.

My job in the squadron was not only to participate in the flying trials, and act as a Squadron Duty Officer, but also as Staff Officer to coordinate all squadron paperwork. The Staff Office consisted of myself and Leading Writer Robilliard (known as Scribes). It was Scribes who did the work of looking after files, typing and generally keeping me straight on Staff Office matters. The major paperwork requirement was to produce a report every month on the Intensive Trials. I had a deadline of Thursday lunchtime for all reports to be into the Staff Office. Scribes and I would get pages into order, do extra typing where it was needed and get the Commanding Officer, Lieutenant Commander Vic Sirett, to approve. The report went to about 120 addresses so once the CO had approved it, it was onto the Gestetner to run off the pages and then to collate, punch holes, and assemble the reports so they were ready to go into the post on Friday morning. Anyone who has familiarity with a Gestetner copier and the black ink required to keep it copying would sympathise with us. Scribes and I would see the sun rising in the East once a month.

During the Autumn of 1969 the CO, was looking for a photograph to headline the Squadron Christmas card.

Close by to Penzance is the village of Madron where the death of Vice Admiral Horatio Nelson at Trafalgar in 1805 was first acknowledged with a memorial ceremony. Folklore has it that HMS PICKLE arrived in Mounts Bay with the news of Nelson's death. A Penzance fishing boat passed the news to shore and his death was announced on the balcony of the Penzance Assembly Rooms. The mother church of Penzance at the time was Madron Parish Church and the Penzance Mayor led a procession to Madron where a memorial service was held. An annual Trafalgar Day service has been held in Madron parish church since 1946.

It may have been Jim Flindell who had the idea for a photograph combining the latest Fleet Air Arm aircraft, the Sea King and a Phantom, overhead Madron church and the planning began. This planning involved the Culdrose Photographic Section, an RNAS Yeovilton Phantom squadron, the vicar of Madron Church et al. In order for the photo to be meaningful it would be necessary for both aircraft to be as close as possible to the church, in the right place at the right time, with the photographer taking the photograph from the right angle. It was planned to get it right first time.

Overleaf you see the photograph that was taken. There is an annotation in the top left by the CO.

What viewers of the photograph are not able to see is the aftermath!

Firstly the Phantom is very low and very slow and is therefore using a lot of power which equals noise. An elderly lady walking up the road to the right with her dog fell to the ground, her dog disappeared and was never seen again. The Phantom is closer than you think and the photographer who was on a scaffold erected for his use, reacted to the noise and the closeness of the aircraft took a step back and the scaffold overturned. The Sea King had taken up its position well in advance of the overflying Phantom, close to the vicarage. The vicarage had not had its chimneys swept for many years and the vibrations caused by the Sea Kings rotors did the job for them. There were reports of farm animals in the vicinity running amok, chickens disappearing never to be seen again and the local community were understood to be less than impressed. Luckily it was planned as a one off run which is just as well for

700S Squadron Sea King HAS Mk 1 cleaning the Madron vicarage chimneys. 1970

Ministry of Defence Crown Copyright 1970

706 Squadron Sea King HAS Mk 1 dropping a torpedo in Falmouth Bay. 1970

Ministry of Defence Crown Copyright 1970

700S Squadron Sea King HAS 1 recovering the sonar body prior to leaving the dip. 1970

Ministry of Defence Crown Copyright 1970

700S Squadron Pilots, Observers and Air Engineering officers. June 1970

Ministry of Defence Crown Copyright 1970

many reasons, one being the recovery of the photographer from his collapsed scaffolding in a hedge.

I am of the mind that there were probably other consequences from this event which have never publicly been revealed. Those are the ones I am aware of.

700(S) completed the Intensive Trials on time and with excellent results. Westland Helicopters showed their gratitude by treating the squadron to a Supper Dance on Friday 29 May 1970. I still have the menu and the signatures of all present recorded on it. Regrettably time has not been kind and many of the signatures have faded and are illegible. This includes the COs line where he declares love for my wife, followed by an apology to Ruth his own wife blaming the wine!

Come the Summer of 1970 and it was time to go back to sea. I was to join HMS BULWARK as Operations Officer 2 but before joining in August I had to complete a Photographic Course at RNAS Lossiemouth as a secondary duty was being the Ships Photographic Officer, and a Joint Warfare Course at RAF Old Sarum.

Chapter 12

RUM

31 JULY 1970

The issue of a rum ration to the Royal Navy began in the 1740s when a quarter of a pint was given to each man, occasionally dosed with lime juice to reduce scurvy. Happily, in the 1850s the amount was reduced to $1/8^{th}$ of a pint with Petty Officers and above receiving their tot neat and Leading Hands and below receiving their $1/8^{th}$ tot mixed with 2/8ths water. The rum was 96.5% proof. Officers were not entitled to a rum ration their ration having been stopped in 1881.

With the advent of the technological age and therefore a need for everyone to be functioning with clear heads, and a realisation that rum was taking up valuable resources and time to administer, the rum ration ceased on 31 July 1970.

On both GRAFTON and ANZIO I had been responsible, as a Duty Officer, for the daily rum issue. That involved drawing the key, and checking the numbers and status of personnel on board; some would be 'G', entitled to their tot (Grog); some would be 'T', that is Temperance, they did not drink their tot and were entitled to a can of beer or lemonade instead; others would be 'UA', that is Under Age, under 20, and therefore not entitled. Having worked all that out the total volume of rum required was drawn from the rum flasks. All the copper measures were checked, the Rum Tub filled and the pipe 'Up Spirits' would be made and the Rum Bosun's from the various Messdecks would appear with their jugs. This was normally around midday. Once the neat spirit and grog had been ladled out there was inevitably some left over which had to be ditched. Rumour has it that in HMS VICTORY, the Portsmouth shore establishment, there was a drain which was kept in a very clean state and was never used for anything else other than the disposal from the Rum Tub. The liquid was spirited away by a series of pipes to a collecting point known only to a select few. Whether or not this is true I have no idea.

On GRAFTON the rum routine worked like clockwork. My memories of rum are all on ANZIO. The rum store on ANZIO was vast as when we had tanks embarked the troops were entitled to their rum the same as the ships company. The Army personnel were not used to this pretty potent drink at lunchtime and when their officers were relaxing in the Wardroom after lunch there would inevitably be a thunderous knocking at the door and a trooper would be there asking to see his officer. The drink would loosen many a tongue after lunch! There were occasions when I managed to mislay the Rum Store key after returning all the gear and locking up. Mysteriously one of the Leading Hands would reappear in the afternoon with the key explaining I had left it in such and such a place. There were many court martials associated with rum and I became a little bit paranoid, but the regular stock takes did not detect any missing rum. I still managed to mislay the rum key up until the day I left.

Young officers would be invited to Mess Decks to sample a tot or two. Mainly to loosen their tongues and to hear them commit a few indiscretions. The rules of 'Gulpers' and 'Sippers' would also be explained.

On rare occasions 'Splice the Mainbrace' can still be ordered by HM the Queen, a member of the Royal Family, or the Admiralty Board, when all personnel above the age of 18 are entitled to a 'tot'. Ships still carry sufficient rum to meet this requirement. Before 1970 that would have meant a double 'tot' to most ratings!

Chapter 13

HMS BULWARK

Operations Officer 2.
August 1970 - September 1972

I joined HMS BULWARK on 24 August 1970 only to find that from September to February 1971 she was going to be in Short Refit in Plymouth Dockyard.

My main responsibility as Operations Officer 2 would be for air operations and briefing aircrew on their missions. I was also the ship's Photographic Officer with a Photographic Section of four RN photographers.

Whilst BULWARK was alongside the Ships Company were able to live onboard. Once BULWARK moved into dry dock the Ships Company moved into HMS DRAKE the shore establishment which provided the naval support and accommodation to units in Plymouth Dockyard. With the ship in dry dock there was still a requirement for a Duty Officer and a Duty Watch onboard overnight for security and emergency reasons. With a very much reduced complement I found myself living onboard overnight almost every other night. It was cold and miserable most of the time, and what surprised me most of all were the number of potential fires I discovered during my night rounds. They would typically be a ball of rags pushed in between pipes or left in a locker with the centre of the ball burning slowly away. The rumour has it that 'dockyard maties' would deliberately leave these 'balls' hidden on ships so that some damage would be caused which would mean the ship would have an extended period in the dockyard therefore giving them more work. I saw no evidence to this effect during my time in refit. Doing rounds in the middle of the night on a deserted ship can be quite challenging as there are noises which it is impossible to identify coming from places that you are not familiar with and all your senses are in play.

Fiona and I attended the Ladies Night Mess Dinner in HMS DRAKE in December 1970. As usual we enjoyed the company, the dinner, and the wine. Although drink-driving was frowned upon, it was not the live issue that it is nowadays. As the rules did not allow wives to stay overnight in the Wardroom, as they do now, it meant that after the dinner I had to drive back to our Married Quarter in Helston, a journey of some 65 miles in the small hours. I am ashamed to admit the following morning I had no recollection whatsoever of that journey back, neither did Fiona. In the days that followed I tried to remember the journey, but never could, and that scared me. I have never driven having had a drink since.

Thankfully BULWARK sailed on Sea Trials without incident, on time, in March 1971 with 845 Squadron (Wessex HU Mk 5) as our embarked squadron and 41 Commando as the embarked force.

In between our work-up and amphibious exercises we visited Stockholm, Helsinki and Liverpool. In July in Liverpool the ship hosted the Liver Birds, Polly James and Nerys Hughes. Their visit was memorable because they had let it be known that after their visit they had to travel down to London on an evening train, - 'Were there any officers who would like to accompany them to dinner in Liverpool before catching the train'. The answer was - 'There are none'. Polly and Nerys left on their own!

In September whilst we were at anchor off Trieste - there was a storm blowing up the Adriatic Sea and no boats had been running inshore. It must have been around 6.30 when there was an explosion in one of the boiler rooms followed by fire. All the alarms were raised and Lieutenant Dave Tink (the Flight Deck Officer) with whom I shared a cabin, and I fell out of our bunks and dressed quickly. We had a visitor in the third bunk, an Army Major, who was onboard for a 'jolly' (a visit with no responsibilities!), who asked was it really necessary for him to get up so early. He got a short sharp answer.

The Commander had taken charge from the Bridge and had assumed the Captain, 'Slug' Notley, was down in HeadQuarters1 (HQ1), the Damage Control Headquarters, in the bowels of the ship. Those who were not involved in fighting the fire were mustering on the Flight Deck and the Quarterdeck, firstly to keep out of the way and secondly to act as a source of manpower should it be required.

I was on the Quarterdeck with several dozen others. It was cold, very cold, and eventually one of the PTIs suggested we start doing physical exercises. So it was running on the spot, star jumps, press-ups etc. By 0900 the fire was under control and everyone was stood down.

What we were not aware of was the Captain, whose cabin was directly beneath the Quarterdeck, had rung the Bridge to ask why there were people doing PT exercises on the Quarterdeck and would they kindly stop so he could get back to sleep (or words to that effect). The Captain had slept through all the alarms, the Commander had assumed he was in HQ1 (from where actions in event of an emergency are controlled). Had we not woken him he would have slept through the entire incident. Regrettably one of the MEs in the boiler room lost his life in the incident and we returned to the UK on one boiler.

The summer of 1972 in the Mediterranean was gorgeous and the latest in the series of NATO exercises were under way in the Aegean Sea. HMS BULWARK was at anchor after a hectic morning's flying. There was to be maximum effort that afternoon in support of the Royal Marines ashore close to the Turkey/Greece border. The ship's company was taking the opportunity to get some sunshine on the flight deck. All the 845 Wessex HU5 had been spotted ready for the big push.

Unusually Lt Cdr(Flying) Lt Cdr Ron Maclean, was manning Flyco (the ship's control tower) over the 'no fly' lunchtime period. Somewhere over the horizon were US fixed wing and helicopter carriers. Peace, perfect peace. Flyco's radio burst into action 'Bulwark, this is Ranger Two Five. Can I have permission to do a pass down your port side in a couple of minutes? Sir, do you have any traffic?

Flyco took in the American accent and assumed this was a Sea Stallion from the US helicopter carrier which had been in the vicinity during the morning. So, no problem: 'Ranger Two Five, no problem, we have no traffic, give me a one minute call'. 'Much obliged sir, and we are one minute to run'

One minute later there was a shattering explosion as one of the USS Ranger's A-5 Vigilante's flew down the port side at Mach 1.5.

Down in the engine and boiler rooms the sound barrier boom sounded like an explosion somewhere within the ship or an aircraft crash on deck. Those on the flight deck and in the hangar were wondering had there been an explosion in the engine/boiler room. On the flight deck the windows and doors of the neatly lined up Wessex HU5 all popped out from the over pressure.

The Operations Room was located just off the flight deck and the closed steel and wooden door was removed from its mountings. I was in the Ops Room preparing for the afternoon briefing. My heart stopped.

For thirty seconds nobody moved, the world stood still, and all those onboard wondered what came next? What did come next? A very sheepish Lt Cdr (Flying) on the Tannoy explaining a fast-flying Vigilante had just flown past in excess of the speed of sound.

HMS Bulwark entering US Naval Base Mayport, Florida. 1971

Ministry of Defence Crown Copyright 1971

During 1972 BULWARK spent a period of 11 weeks anchored in Grand Harbour, Malta. This was a period of strained relationships between Malta and the UK caused mainly by Dom Mintoff the Maltese Prime Minister elected in 1971, attempting to re-negotiate the post-independence military and financial agreements. The ships company was warned that any bad behaviour ashore would not be tolerated.

HMS Bulwark at Assault Stations somewhere in the Mediterranean. (1971)

Ministry of Defence Crown Copyright 1971

HMS Bulwark firmly secured in Valetta Harbour, Malta. Note: Wessex HU Mk 5 positioned just aft of the island. 1971

Ministry of Defence Crown Copyright 1971

One evening a group of us decided to proceed ashore and have a few drinks in a bar in the St Georges area. None of us had been there before, but it came recommended. I seem to remember there was around eight of us. The bar was deserted and Lieutenant Jimmy James (a very talented Meteorological Officer) and I occupied a couple of stools at the bar, whilst the remainder sat around a table. The bar tender/owner turned out to be an unusual character being British, but had taken out Maltese citizenship. We chatted over a drink and Jimmy accidently slipped off his stool, but not because he had had too much to drink. I laughed, he got back on his stool and pushed me off mine. The others were engaged in earnest conversations.

Minutes later Tim Yarker on his way back from the heads (toilets) saw the Naval Patrol arrive outside looking business like. He alerted the others at their table and they quickly and quietly made their way out through the second exit. The next thing Jimmy and I were aware of was two burly Naval Patrolmen standing behind us inviting us to accompany them back to BULWARK. How could we refuse!

The following morning Jimmy and I were 'invited' to 'sliding door' interviews with the Commander. The Commander normally kept his cabin sliding door open. If it was closed it was for a reason!

The bar owner had feared that he was going to have trouble with this group from BULWARK. The acts of slipping and being pushed off the bar stools confirmed his worse fears and he had immediately phoned for the Naval Patrol. Commander Parry only half believed our story, but he did not stop our shore leave.

In the accompanying photograph of BULWARK in Grand Harbour on the starboard side of the flight deck there is a parked Wessex HU5. I believe this may be one of 845 Squadron aircraft which ditched but was retrieved from the water very quickly. On my daily walk from my cabin to the Operations Office I would walk past this aircraft and listen to the 'crinkling sounds' coming from it. Magnesium and sea water do not mix well and the sea water was gradually eating away the fabric of the aircraft despite all efforts to stop it.

It was time to get back to aviation and because of my service in 700(S) Squadron I was appointed to the Sea King Simulator at RNAS Culdrose. From a family point of view this was excellent news.

Chapter 14

RNAS CULDROSE

Officer in Charge Sea King Simulator.
September 1972 – February 1974

This was an appointment that I approached with some trepidation. It was a pure training job for which I was unsure as to whether I had the right temperament. However, after a couple of months I began to enjoy the training role and gained the confidence that I needed to do the job well.

As Officer in Charge (OIC) I was responsible for the simulator training of all Sea King Pilots, Observers and Aircrewmen and this included the foreign Navies that were going through Culdrose, the German Navy, Indian Navy and Pakistani Navy. From time to time there were also Norwegian and Danish crews who came to complete 'emergencies' training that could not be replicated in the air. Lieutenant Commander Colin Young was responsible for the pilot training and his support to me was critical to giving all front line and foreign aircrew the training they required.

Teaching radar theory to the Pakistani crews was challenging as when you ask if they have understood, the response is a shake of the head not a nod!

The Simulator consisted of a single fully motion enabled Sea King front end for pilot training and a single back seat cabin with no motion facilities. The front seat and back seat facilities could be electronically linked to become one aircraft or operate independently for training. The instructor's consoles gave complete control over all inputs from the engines to the radar and sonar. The instructors consoles also acted as other units cooperating with the aircrew in the simulator.

Within the obvious limitations of the simulator we attempted to make things as realistic as possible. On one sortie being conducted with a German crew they argued between themselves to the extent that they had fisticuffs once the sortie was over!

The simulator was maintained by Link Miles a company based in Shoreham. There were three engineers on site responsible for keeping us serviceable. Every two months myself, Colin and the senior engineer attended a maintenance/improvements meeting in the Link Miles premises at Shoreham. It was a welcome couple of days away from the pressure of the simulator. I never managed to achieve one of my goals which was to have a 'voice changer' at the instructors console so that other units could be more realistically simulated. I am sure the crews under training hated the same voice pretending to be another Sea King or a frigate, and it would have helped with misunderstandings.

Backseat simulator staff consisted of myself and Chief Aircrewman Paul Johnston. Colin and another pilot, with occasionally a third pilot who was medically unfit but could be usefully employed, completed the instructional staff. Long days were worked as we aimed to fill every available simulator slot.

One month was so busy to the extent that I was only able to get across to the Wardroom to buy cigarettes. At the end of that month I received a Mess Bill of £45 of which over £40 was cigarettes. I realised I could use that monthly £40 to pay off a new car (second-hand!). I stopped smoking the day I received the Mess Bill and have never smoked since.

Link Miles requested, Colin and myself to accompany them on a sales trip to the Danish Air Force in Copenhagen, all expenses paid. A very enjoyable couple of days but no sales to the Danes!

As a fixed resource at Culdrose which was quite visual we would be asked to host all manner of visitors to the simulator which I like to think we all took in our stride.

In the late summer of 1973 the Flag Officer Naval Air Command (FONAC) organised a Fleet Air Arm wide Escape and Evasion exercise on Dartmoor. Every Fleet Air Arm aircrew member in the UK was ordered to attend, no excuses were accepted. The Hunter Force was 42 Royal Marines Commando based at Bickleigh just outside Plymouth. The exercise involved teams of five setting out from Okehampton Army Camp on Friday afternoon having been given five rendezvous points around Dartmoor which they would check in with, ending up in Okehampton Camp by Sunday evening. There were to be over 500 aircrew involved. I was given a team to lead which included Paul Johnston, a Lieutenant whose name I seem to remember was David, and two other aircrew from a Culdrose based squadron. My reader may remember I had vowed never to be caught by Royal Marines on an Escape and Evasion exercise ever again! A plan was hatched.

My team arrived at Okehampton Camp by coach on the Friday and it was a bit like a reunion party, meeting oppos we had not seen for years. The FONAC staff who were attempting to administer this throng of aircrew had their job cut out. Eventually teams set off onto Dartmoor at five minute intervals making for the first rendezvous point. As pre-arranged the two other aircrew disappeared within 30 minutes of us leaving the camp to meet up with another group. Paul, Lt D and myself plodded on into the night to rendezvous point one. We had worked out that the RMs would not be trying to catch anyone at this early stage in the exercise and headed directly to point one. We checked in and continued to our next stop. Dartmoor is not the best place to try and cross at night with the going either flat and stony or full of pools of water and marsh. We eventually arrived in a small area of bracken and bushes overlooking the B3242 running between Princetown and Mortonhampstead. We got under cover as much as we could and lay down to wait. We did see Royal Marine Landrovers travelling on the road. Mid-afternoon our transport arrived in the shape of Lt D's wife and her car and we were transported to Lt Ds home south of the moor. They had a caravan in the garden in which Paul and I spent the Saturday night. Sunday lunch was in the local very small pub with the locals looking at us curiously in our dirty flying suits.

Late Sunday afternoon it was into the car for the journey back to Okehampton Camp. There was a small track which went around the back of Okehampton Camp where we could be dropped, climb over fence and once in the camp we were on safe ground according to the rules. Just getting dark we could see the lights of the camp, no-one around, out of the car and across some moorland, over the fence and we were safe. We made our way to the check-in point. All of a sudden from behind us we heard a shout of 'Halt' and feet running down the road, Lt D and I took to our feet like the wind and sped to the check in building bursting through the double doors simultaneously with such force that we smashed one of the panes of glass in the doors. Turning round we could see that Paul was being hauled away by three Marines. I complained to the FONAC staff about this breaking of the rules as the camp was safe ground. Luckily one of the staff officers listened, went outside and ordered the Marines to release Paul, which they did. We checked in and then joined the coach to take us back to Culdrose.

To fill in some gaps in the story. The Commando that was the Hunter Force were due to go on an overseas deployment in a week's time. To a man they were unhappy that their last weekend before deploying had been taken up with chasing aircrew across Dartmoor when they could have been on pre-deployment leave. The rumour went around the Fleet Air Arm contingent that anyone 'captured' during the exercise was not going to have an easy time. Accordingly, small groups made their plans.

By Saturday lunchtime it had become obvious that there were virtually no aircrew within the exercise area. Although most groups had made rendezvous point one there was a scarcity of checking in at the rest. In the week that followed the exercise stories began to circulate. Bed and Breakfast businesses in Holsworthy, South Molton and other small towns to the north of Dartmoor had seen an increase in bookings. Garages had been rented in Okehampton and people had slept in their cars inside the garages. One person had attended a wedding in Torquay. There were many stories circulating and the one that got most attention was that FONAC himself had received a post card from Torquay saying 'Wish you Here'.

I have no doubt that the Commando had also made a strong representation to FONAC about the lack of escapees on Dartmoor.

The upshot was that everyone involved had to give their 'reasons in writing' to FONAC describing their actions during the exercise. As can be imagined there were small groups gathering throughout the Fleet Air Arm estate engaged in creative writing. Paul, Lt D and I put together a tale about the Hunter Force surrounding the rendezvous points so that we were unable to check in, but we bravely completed the course and were pounced upon as we entered the camp. We later learnt that some groups were not so lucky and had been 'captured' within the camp, then transported to Bickleigh for an unpleasant experience at the hands of the Royal Marines.

To my knowledge no action was ever taken over what turned out as a debacle.

Just before Christmas, and out of the blue, my next appointment was suggested, an Exchange posting in the South of France. Sounds wonderful but with two young daughters at school, a son just about to go to school, and a family Labrador we had to think quickly and carefully. The two daughters were in a boarding school and could come out for holidays; our son could start his schooling in France and would have a good attribute to take back to the UK, his French language skills; and one of the Simulator staff volunteered to look after our Labrador whilst we were away. We decided to go to France.

Chapter 15

BAN ST MANDRIER

31F Flottille/Wessex HSS1.
March 1974 – March 1976

Lieutenant Keith Wyman (P) and myself (O) were selected for the exchange posting with 31F Flottille based at Base Aeronavale (BAN) St Mandrier close to Toulon in the south of France.

Neither Keith nor I were French speaking, neither of us were aware of the posts, nor had we volunteered! The RN arranged language tuition. This consisted of a week in London at a language school in Oxford Street. It was very loosely called a language school as we spent three mornings under tuition; afternoons were private study as the tutor went off to see his mistress. The final two days were again private study!

Our exchange started with a visit to the Naval Attache in Paris, Captain Bird. Both families stayed in the French Naval Officers Club, the Cercle Navale, in central Paris, with parking and very cheap. After meeting Captain Bird and receiving our brief from the Admin Staff the six of us, (Keith and Shirley had a babe in arms and we had John our four year old), found a small restaurant for lunch. Shirley went off to the ladies. Seconds later there was a scream and Shirley reappeared at the table vowing never to visit here again. Shirley had discovered the 'elephant feet' toilet.

The next day we set out on our respective routes to the South of France. Keith went straight down on the autoroute and we took the country route, stopping overnight at Le Puy. The snow covered roads in and around Le Puy were interesting and I was relieved when we finally rejoined the autoroute to Marseilles in bright Spring sunshine.

I was relieving John Madgewick and we would be taking over the flat that he and his wife Pippa were living in. We lived cheek by jowl for a week during the handover.

Keith and I thought it would be a good idea to 'break the ice' with 31F so we organised an evening soiree with drinks and small eats for the Squadron and their wives. Keith and Shirley were living in a house with more room than our flat so that was selected as the venue. As space was going to be a problem we took all the chairs out of the ground floor, leaving tables for drink and food. Most of the Squadron turned up plus their wives but within an hour or so they all started to leave and within ninety minutes it was just the four of us left. The next day everyone said thank you and they enjoyed it! It was only several weeks later that we were to learn people had left early because there was nowhere for them to sit and chat. There were other cultural differences; for example just dropping in on other Squadron families was not encouraged – you had to be invited. There was no point in knocking on anyone's door after 2000, they would not answer. But there were advantages to our new life in France; local markets; the weather; and the travel we were able to do. We met the local Lloyds Shipping Insurance engineer. His patch extended from Gibraltar to the toe of Italy. He and his wife lived in a truly beautiful house overlooking the Mediterranean awaiting the next call to do an engineering insurance assessment somewhere in his patch. His wife had spent three years doing French at university but said she was unable to converse with the French because they did not understand her! We camped with the children throughout France with vivid memories of our first night with our first tent on a beach at Cavalaire with a violent Mediterranean storm raging and all of us hanging onto the tent structure to stop it being blown away.

Base Aeronavale (BAN) St Mandrier, Toulon. 31F Flotille hangar and building are on the right of the picture. 1974

Keith applied himself to the French language and very quickly became fluent. I struggled to the extent that sometime after my arrival in France I brought the matter up with the Naval Attache, Captain Bird. He discovered that my French equivalent on exchange in UK was also having a language problem and had been sent to Bournemouth for a language course. He promptly arranged for me to attend a language course with the Institute de Francais in Villefranche sur Mer, just to the East of Nice. Captain Bird had undergone his language training at the Institute and had made friends with the owner. After one month of training the owner recommended to Captain Bird that I would benefit from a second month, which was approved! The training was excellent; nothing other than French during the working day and very much the spoken word rather than anything written. I suppose the highlights were the other people on the course. Too many to remember all of them but a cross-section included, Susannah Sandeman (heiress to Sandemans Port); an American couple from Alaska who made their money from renting out land for accommodation huts to oil companies; a 'gentleman' who made his money from scamming people using 'the Dover Plan' and was wanted in UK for fraud (he arrived every day in his Rolls Royce and needed French to be able to converse with his housekeeper); a businessman from Canada told by his accountant he should spend money otherwise he would lose it in tax (his ballet dancer wife was dancing in Vienna whilst he did his course). There was a lot of eating out during the course and us 'poorer' members seldom paid anything towards the cost. A view into how the other half lived!

One of the squadron highlights each year was the annual ditching drill qualification in the warm waters of the Mediterranean. This was undertaken in the French equivalent of the 'dunker' at RNAS Yeovilton known as 'La Glotte'.

La Glotte consisted of a steel shell configured as the rear cabin of the HSS-1 (a piston engine Wessex). During the year it rested behind the St Mandrier hangers, and for one week it emerged to sit alongside the St Mandrier 'runway which ran alongside Toulon harbour. La Glotte was attached to an ancient mobile crane.

French helicopter aircrew were supplied with an underwater breathing apparatus which would provide a few minutes of air in the event of a ditching and this training gave aircrew confidence in the use of this equipment.

Training consisted of a number of runs in different seats, with and without the breathing apparatus, with blindfold or without. For each run the ancient mobile crane would lift La Glotte, suspend it over the harbour, release, and once settled on the bottom the occupants would escape.

But life in 31F was never simple. Over the years a tradition had emerged that the entire squadron, or as many as could be crammed into La Glotte would be loaded and dropped into the Mediterranean. The last aircrew member to emerge being the winner. Neither Keith nor I were aware of this as we were invited for the n'th time to take up position in the steel shell. As body after body piled in I began to have doubts about this run. The ancient mobile crane had obviously reached the limit of its capacity as we swung out over the water and it must have sighed with relief as we plunged down towards the bottom.

My thoughts fluctuated from 'this is a mass drowning' or 'is it just a bad dream', especially as when we reached the bottom nobody moved. Eventually someone moved, and very slowly, and gradually bodies exited the door and windows but with no urgency. By this time my instinct, reinforced by a lack of air, was to get out – quickly. As I left through a window I could see bodies clinging on, so although they had left the interior they were still hanging on hoping to be the last to surface. So ended another day in 31F, another memory etched in my mind.

During our time in 31F we embarked in FNS CLEMENCEAU (French aircraft carrier). Keith and I flew to Brest with the ground party in a French Air Force Transall and embarked in CLEMENCEAU. It was a short deployment from 5 to 21 May and involved going from Brest, around the Canary Islands and back to Brest. We went to Action Stations every afternoon, but only for 15 minutes. Flying was hardly intense. My major excitement was to be woken at 0530 and called to the bridge to identify ships in a Russian Task Force which the French Task Force was approaching. Ship recognition was a skill which the RN put high on the agenda, the French Navy did not. I could not believe the bridge were uncertain about what they were fast approaching. I was able to do the necessary identification and the French Admiral ordered the French Task Force to continue on its course which took it directly across the path of the Russian ships. The result was the Russian ships had to take evasive action. As far as I could ascertain there was no radio contact between the two forces. This is unusual as between RN and Russian naval vessels there would be communication to avoid any misunderstandings.

Anti-submarine exercises tended to be very basic and would be cancelled with little justification. Keith and I never flew together.

31F Flotille HSS-1. HMS Norfolk can just be seen leaving Toulon Harbour. The Glotte. Immersing. Emerging.

Author's photos 1975

There were navigation sorties into the Alps Maritime with various mountain tops to place a wheel on. A sortie through the Gorges of Verdun was memorable due to the fact that it was a prohibited area since rock falls had been caused by aircraft activity. Here we were, below the tops of the gorge, to all intents just sight-seeing, and causing who knows what rocks to fall behind us. A Gallic shrug was the response to my question, why did we do that?

Every two years a meeting was held in the British Embassy in Paris for RN, RAF & Army officers on exchange with the French forces. Captain Bird, the Naval Attachee, organised a lunch with the Free French Club some distance from the Embassy. I sat next to a French gentleman and listened to his wartime story. Escaping from the French coast in a trawler he landed in Falmouth. He was trained and returned to France as part of the Resistance movement and spent time blowing up trains and railways. All the RN exchange officers were deep into this lunch and hearing fascinating stories from our hosts. We managed to overstay our welcome by at least an hour and had to run through the streets of Paris to get back to the Embassy to find we had missed half of the afternoon's events.

Whilst serving in 31F, I wrote an article for the Fleet Air Arm Safety Magazine which you will find at the end of this chapter. It was written with my tongue firmly in my cheek. Meeting one of the 31F French pilots who was serving in the French Embassy in London at a joint RN/Marine Nationale meeting in 1985 I was to learn that the article had found its way to 31F and the Commanding Officer was incandescent for the next few days. Luckily, I was far away by then.

On our arrival in France we had taken over the flat from John Madgewick in Tamaris. The flat was the upstairs apartment in a house owned by a Greek dentist and his wife who lived downstairs. The dentist also had his wartime story to tell. He had been working in Paris when the Germans invaded and he remained in the city continuing to do dentistry. To cut a long story short, he eventually had clients of German officers using his dental expertise. He was approached by the Resistance and asked to pass information back to them. There was an event where precision bombing, literally through the window, resulted to the death of a high ranking German officer, which he ascribed to the information that he had passed to the Resistance. He lived through interesting times.

Very close to where we lived was a Napoleonic fort on the top of a hill called strangely enough Fort Napoleon. Fort Napoleon and its counterpoint across the Toulon Harbour entrance, the Royal Tower, would have guarded the entrance to Toulon Harbour. Fort Napoleon was totally abandoned, there was no organisation looking after it and I spent a lot of time just wandering through the fort and imagining what life would have been like in its heyday.

Although the Tamaris flat was pleasant and our landlord very accommodating there was not enough room to get our two daughters out to stay during their school holidays. We moved out to a flat in Six Fours les Plages with three bedrooms. It was a good move as we made friends with a Dutch couple, Ann and Gilbert. Ann spoke five European languages including Polish. We made an acquaintance with a French couple, the extremely large and powerfully built husband being a former French Legionnaire and we saw photos of him holding a large and ancient cannon barrel in his hands as though it was a rifle. Inexplicitly he committed suicide by blowing his head off with a shotgun in his car very close to our balcony.

Through John's school we met an Irish author, Ian Gibson and his wife who lived just across the road from our apartment. I am afraid there were some very boozy evenings. Ian's claim to fame was his book entitled 'The Death of Lorca'. My copy of his book is inscribed 'For James and Fiona (with a shaky hand), Best Wishes, Six-Fours, 29 Jan 1976' The inscription was written as the sun was coming up on another day in the South of France. He spent a lot of time in the UK and Italy in connection with a film to be made about the Spanish poet Lorca.

But all good things come to an end and news came through that I was to return to the UK, do a refresher course and join 824 Squadron. We had enjoyed our time in France but we were glad to be returning to UK.

Our journey back from France at the end of my appointment is worth recording. Fiona, John (now aged 6) and I set out in our Austin 3 litre with a small trailer on a Thursday morning in late

March 1976. All was well until south of Lyon on the A6 autoroute the engine started to lose power. I pulled into a service station, opened the bonnet and there was engine oil everywhere.

I called the autoroute emergency services. They appeared quite quickly and said they would tow us to the nearest garage. The recovery truck continued north towards Lyon turning off short of Lyon into what we took to be a scrap yard. Our thoughts can only be imagined.

Despite appearances it did have garage facilities and was the Citroen/Maserati agent for the Lyon area. It did not take them long to diagnose the problem; the piston rings had given up and the pressure had forced engine oil out into the engine bay. The Austin 3 litre was not a recognised car in France and the required spares were not available in France. I was not a member of the AA or RAC. So the garage mechanic gave me a list of the spares I would need for them to do a repair.

After looking at various options I sped into Lyon by taxi to the AVIS van and car hire office and hired a Peugeot van which was big enough to take the trailer inside. Back to the scrap yard, load the trailer and head back to England to locate the spares. On Thursday night, instead of being in a hotel in Paris followed by a courtesy call on the Naval Attache next day, we were driving direct to Calais to catch a ferry. The heater in the Peugeot van was not working so it was a cold journey.

Our original intention had been to spend a few days with my parents at Upton before travelling down to Cornwall to move into a Married Quarter in Helston on the Friday. But we arrived a little earlier than expected on Friday lunchtime. Upton is south of Oxford where Austin/Morris cars were made and I spent the Friday afternoon and Saturday morning ringing up various garages for the spare parts that I required. By the time I had located them all it was Saturday afternoon and no chance of collecting them that day. Early on the Monday morning I set off to drive around the various garages in Oxford collecting the parts before setting off for Dover. I caught a late evening ferry to Calais.

It must have been about ten o'clock when I left Calais and there was a hitch-hiker looking for a lift. I intended to drive straight to Lyon and thought the hitch-hiker will help me stay awake. I assumed he was French and he assumed I was French (driving a French van!). My French was more than passable at this point in time. After about an hour I discovered that he was Canadian and we gave up speaking French and conversed in English. His presence was invaluable as it kept me awake as we drove towards Lyon.

I drove into the scrap yard in the morning just as the mechanics were stirring. They confirmed they now had all the right bits and would get onto the job right away. The advice I had had from the garages in Oxford was that the engine would have to be removed in order to effect the repairs and this might be a two day job. I returned the Peugeot van to Lyon and on arrival back at the scrap yard the owner offered to take me for lunch. We got into his Citroen SM, a three seat sports car, and drove down a straight road parallel to the autoroute. On this straight road was a small bridge with high sides requiring a 45 degree turn to get onto and exit the bridge. It was not possible to see what was coming from the other direction. We took the bridge at about 60/70 mph and over lunch I asked why he took the bridge at such a speed. His logic was that the odds of someone coming from the other direction meeting him in the short time he was on the bridge were negligible. My brain was too tired to argue.

Back after lunch I lay down on the rear seat of the Austin and slept. I was awoken at six o'clock with the news that the job was complete. The piston rings and all the other things that had to be changed had been fitted without taking the engine out. A minor miracle as far as I was concerned.

Back onto the road and taking it easy to allow the repairs to settle in, I drove towards Paris. I had arranged to visit the Naval Attachee on the Wednesday morning. In fact he was away. However I still had administrative matters to settle with his staff before heading for Calais. I was now in the third day with little sleep and in the same clothes.

Paris visit over I headed for Calais feeling more confident with the car. I arrived at Upton late on the Wednesday night looking for a shower and a bed! On Thursday we drove down to Cornwall to move into the Married Quarter on the Friday. I had covered 2426 miles in seven days and was quite glad to settle down to a new routine at Culdrose.

I was sad to learn BAN St Mandrier was shut and sold in 2014. It is now a very high class Marina and Yacht Repair Yard. The runway now has a line-up of very expensive motor boats and yachts on it.

'ELLOW! 'ELLOW.' MON AMI —
AM JE CLE-ARE Too JOHN?

PARLEZ VOUS LE FRANCAIS?

OR `MY FRIEND WILL PAY´

By Lieutenant J. M. MILNE

Contrary to popular opinion and COCKPIT Issue No.74 in the Article "As the General was saying . . ." the Exchange Officers in France do not spend all their time sleeping in the Crewroom—we do it on the beaches!! However in between naps we manage to fly and to read COCKPIT.

The above mentioned article raised some points on a subject which has been a bone of contention in the Fleet Air Arm for a very long time, even longer than Lieutenant Commander TINK has been in the Air Arm. Possibly a few more "logs to the fire" from France might help those at the "sharp end" to persuade the Staff to give us a reasonable fit.

What do the Aeronavale have as a Radio Fit in their helicopters? Both UHF and VHF dialable and preset, a Radio Compass, TACAN and IFF. HF is not fitted, as normally the operating radius of the aircraft does not warrant it.

Not a bad Radio Fit and it does enable the aircraft to go anywhere at any time.

Of course the Aeronavale has its own little problems. One little piece of equipment they would like to have is a UHF Homer. Happily this will appear in the French version of the LYNX.

Another source of irritation is the "cold mike" system. Trials on a "hot mike" system have been carried out, but nothing has been yet said as to what the outcome may be. The Radio Compass is used rarely as the TACAN is used as the main navigation aid. (Most French ships carry TACAN). So far as the French are concerned they have a good basic fit, all that is lacking are the refinements such as the UHF Homer.

The Frenchman operating in France on both civil and Military sides does not therefore have too many problems, but let me now turn to the British Service pilot carrying out his first landaway or doing a Casevac from a Leander to an airfield in France.

No problem! just boom in and talk to the Tower, the International Air Traffic Control Language is English!

Correct, but in France it is French English. French Air Traffic Controllers are in the main, taught their English by other Frenchmen. What, to a Frenchman teaching English may sound perfect, would, to an English ear, sound merely like a garble of words. So you arrive at the situation where the responses from the Tower or Ground Station are word perfect,

14

difficult as may be first imagined. Think of yourself as Maurice Chevalier with bone-dome and cyclic instead of hat and cane, and in no time the French accent will be rolling forth from the tongue. The result may have your crew rolling in the aisles, but the effect in the ground station will be instant recognition of what you are saying, reducing by half the confusion mentioned earlier. Your own brain will also attune itself better to receiving the Frenchified English of the reply.

Another factor to remember when speaking to French Military Ground Stations is that almost everyone you speak to on the R/T will be a Senior Rate, possibly even a Junior Rate. Do not expect an instant answer to any question which is in any way out of the ordinary. The question may have to be referred through two or three other people before you get an answer.

Having arrived finally at your destination there are a few points to watch. Your marshaller will be without ear defenders and probably not covered up. Whilst

. . . . "The question may have to be referred through two or three other people" . . . . .

but the sound one expects to hear is different and confusion starts to set in.

Conversely the French Controller is looking for calls in English with a French accent and he similarly will have to translate the pure English that he hears into English with a French accent. All this takes time and the Flight Safety problem is already becoming apparent.

What is the answer?

The first and simplest answer is to speak French. No problem if you happen to be an A1 French Interpreter. However, it is no good if the only French you know is "my friend will pay".*

If you say two words in French, the Controller will immediately assume that you are conversant with his language and start a conversation with you about the England/France rugby match, the price of garlic and all those other things very close to a Frenchman's heart/stomach.

The second method and by far the best is to speak your English with a French accent. This is not as

. . . . "Your marshaller will be without ear defenders and probably not covered up" . . . .

15

you shut down, at least two or three people will walk through the rotor disc and sit on your flotation canisters.

Be very much aware of these things.

The bowser driver and refuelling team will arrive and probably light up during refuelling (after offering you one first!).

During lunch you will be offered copious amounts of wine to drink. This is not to get you drunk so that your flight back will be a memorable one but French hospitality. The best thing to do is to take a "token" $\frac{1}{2}$ inch (Eds note 12.5mm) of red wine in your glass and top it right up with water. This is the accepted thing to do and satisfies everyone. You have tasted

their necks. They will stay at a respectful distance and just look and talk. Hangar pilots do not appear to exist in France. If you have time to spare on your return to your aircraft then is the time to further Anglo/French relations. Invite some of them to have a look around. They might not understand what you are saying and vice versa, but you will have satisfied the curious and done a small piece of Public Relations work at the same time.

To sum up—one off and unscheduled trips to France can be done just as easily as in UK provided you plan ahead with your radio calls, adapt your English to the French language and accept that answers to your questions may not be forthcoming at the normal speed.

. . . "that deceptively small Armagnac after the meal has deadly effects" . . . .

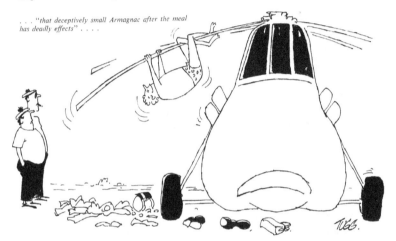

the wine, albeit just red tinged water and you have accepted their hospitality.

Try out your French at this stage, it will be appreciated by all concerned. Avoid talking about NATO or joking about Italian wine or General DE GAULLE. Irish jokes go down very well, but make your Irishmen into Belgians! Lunch will go on for about $2\frac{1}{2}$ hours so do not plan on a quick stop, the quick lunch is unknown in France.

Your aircraft, meanwhile, will be a centre of attraction on the hardstanding. Don't worry about it. You will not return to find it covered in beret-clad Frenchmen, smoking Gauloise and carrying onions round

Accept French hospitality, but remain well within your own capabilities, that deceptively small Armagnac after the meal has deadly effects if you are not used to it! Spread a little bit of Public Relations around, language is not so much of a barrier if people are interested.

Now, what was I talking about?

Ah yes, Radio Fits in aircraft.

Well, Need I mention that, in order to visit "La France" and to be assured of good communications, you need to carry both UHF and VHF! Bon Voyage!!

*PS My friend will pay—Mon ami va payer.

16

Chapter 16

824 SQUADRON/SEA KING HAS 1

HMS ARK ROYAL.
June 1976 – November 1978

Following a refresher course on Wessex 3 and Sea King HAS 1 aircraft I joined 824 Squadron in Norfolk, USA, embarked in HMS ARK ROYAL, in June 1976, and was appointed Senior Observer in October. This was to be HMS ARK ROYAL's final commission and there was service in home waters, the eastern Atlantic and the Mediterranean.

Life was busy, full of Combined Anti-Submarine Exercises (CASEXs), embarkations on Royal Fleet Auxiliaries (RFAs), and large scale NATO exercises in both the North Atlantic and Mediterranean.

824 was a typical eight aircraft anti-submarine Sea King squadron. Headed by a Lieutenant Commander Commanding Officer, wth second in command either the Senior Pilot (SPLOT) or Senior Observer (SOBS) and an Air Engineering Officer (AEO). Then followed the Qualified Helicopter Flying Instructor (QFI) responsible for flying standards, the Helicopter Warfare Instructor (HWI) and finally a whole plethora of SLJOs (Silly Little Jobs Officers). There was a Squadron Direction Officer who manned the ships radar during squadron operations thus giving us confidence by communicating with one of 'our own'. The CO, SPLOT, SOBS and AEO were known as 'Wheels' and when the squadron was flying one of the 'Wheels' (standfast the AEO) would be immediately available for advice to Cdr(Air) in

the event there was an airborne emergency involving a squadron aircraft. Commander (Air) was responsible for the conduct of air operations from the carrier and his Deputy, Lt Cdr(Flying) known as Little F, was responsible for circuit and deck operations such as launch and recovery which was managed from the Flying Control Position (FLYCO).

The SOBS would be responsible for ahead planning and with SPLOT would plan the flying programme for the following day or in the case of NATO exercises for the next fortnight. All aircrew would be involved in flying duties plus the 'Wheels' on duty in Flyco and all other aircrew being Squadron Duty Officer (SDO) for 24 hours, in effect being responsible for running the squadron Flying Programme (FLYPRO). Being SDO was no sinecure in a Strike Carrier being seemingly at the beck and call of the Squadron Wheels, Lt Cdr Flying, the Squadron AEO, the Flight Deck Officer, Uncle Tom Cobley and all, whilst negotiating engine runs between launches, finding a pilot to do the engine run, changing crews over because someone has gone sick. It was never-ending. And what had you to look forward to? Slotting back into the FLYPRO once your 24 hours was over!

But it was not all work and no play. Whilst in port there was a chance to relax. On a visit to Hamburg in October 1977 there was an invitation to a party at the University of Hamburg for 30 officers. Well, those places were soon filled with a reserve list a mile long. The Commander stepped in. He ruled that only Midshipmen and Sub Lieutenants were eligible. If there were any spare places then Lieutenants could add their name. The evening arrived, there was transport from the jetty, and the eager young officers were off to the University. The next morning the truth unfolded. The university was closed and the students all away. In their absence the dining facilities were annually made available to a reunion of a group of ex WW2 German Navy Officers. This group thought it made sense to invite Royal Navy officers to what turned out to be a very boozy evening with lots of good German food, beer and singing. Our young officers put on a good face and

824 Squadron Sea King HAS 1 winching training on HMS ARK ROYAL flight deck. 1976

Ministry of Defence Crown Copyright 1976

all said it was an enjoyable evening, but not quite what they had expected!

The Commander on VICTORIOUS, the ship's Second in Command, was the President of the Wardroom. In effect, he was the organisations Chairman, responsible for all that went on within the Wardroom. He was not an overly popular officer as he spent most of his time refusing to allow things to happen to the extent that he became known as BEANO. There will <u>be no</u> singing, there will <u>be no</u> drinking etc. He had such a thing about drinking that he examined every officer's drink mess-bill at the end of each month. He considered aircrew drank most, so he would invite the squadron COs to a meeting and bring to their attention who he thought were the problem drinkers. This stopped after the meeting when he demanded to know 'who is this fellow Buckley who appears to be drinking far too much?' 'This fellow Buckley' just happened to be our CO, Lieutenant Commander Peter Buckley, who was present. The Commander's people skills were not the best!

Following the Mediterranean deployment with a stop in Toulon a decision was made to fly three Squadron aircraft back to the UK from Toulon. Leaving on 18 October, arriving back in the UK on 20 October with night stops at the French Air Force Base at Cognac and Aeronavale Base at Landivisiau in Brittany. For those selected to make the trip it was the chance to get their kit and 'rabbits' back home early. 'Rabbits' are presents for those back home. A 'rabbit run ' was a dedicated trip ashore to buy those presents. A limit was put on how much baggage each person was entitled to load into the aircraft. Lieutenant Dave Hutchinson and Lieutenant Bob Green were my pilots for the trip back and carefully checked the baggage onboard. Due to Ark Royal's position in the Toulon Naval Dockyard it was necessary to do a 'towering take off' from the deck before gaining forward movement and speed. Take off at 0900 was uneventful and we set off across the Gulf of Lions towards Carcassone for a refuelling stop. About an hour into the flight Bob Green said that he had just calculated that we were now down to Maximum All Up Weight and we could all relax. The rest of the trip was uneventful; we refuelled at Carcassone in the pouring rain; we were very well looked after at the French Air Force Base at Cognac with transport to a local hostelry for a great French evening meal. We arrived back at Culdrose at 1500 on the 20 Oct.

Now back in Culdrose I was giving the CO, Dave Anderson, a lift back home. I had traded in the petrol drinking Austin 3 Litre and now had a Mini Traveller. I was taking a short cut on the smaller

Cornish lanes which were lined with 'Cornish hedges'. Cornish hedges are not hedges in the normal sense. They are small walls built up over many years and which, with the greenery attached, do not look solid. As we came to a very narrow part of the road I espied a Fiesta coming towards us at a speed incompatible with the conditions! I braked and stopped. Within seconds of stopping we were hit front on by the oncoming Fiesta and knocked backwards. Out of the car stepped a lady whose first words were 'Oh no, not again'. She obviously made a habit of crashing/speeding in Cornish lanes. Because of those words my insurance claim was met in full.

1978 was equally busy with detachments to RFAs, CASEXs, torpedo drops, depth charge drops from RNAS Culdrose; and from HMS ARK ROYAL, a Joint Maritime Course (JMC) involving NATO and foreign forces, two major exercises, Ocean Safari (North Atlantic) and Iles d'Or 77 (Mediterranean)

I liked to keep the squadron active so organised an escape and evasion exercise around Cape Wrath, with limited numbers selected out of the hat. My name came out of the hat by sleight of hand, as I discovered later. I had ended up on a survival exercise on Vieques in the Caribbean by the same method!

The squadron disembarked three aircraft from Royal Fleet Auxiliary OLMEDA to Bergen airfield in Norway for an exercise in the Norwegian Sea and were accommodated in the Norwegian submarine base close to Bergen. Drink is extremely expensive in Norway so it was thought prudent to take our own supplies of beer and lager. On arrival in the accommodation I was the only one given a cabin on my own and which had the capacity to store the crates. I literally had to climb over the crates to get out of my door. Just after lunch on our first afternoon in the Norwegian submariners Wardroom we heard the sound of breaking glass on the road outside. This happened at regular intervals. On enquiring we found out that when a Norwegian submarine came back off patrol it was the custom to hold a party in the upstairs rooms. Once a bottle had been opened, it had to be drunk and then disposed of out the window. To the other inhabitants of the Wardroom this was normal behaviour and the glass was picked up by the crew after their party. We paid a visit to one of their ten man patrol submarines during our stay and as a result we totally understood why the crew threw their end of patrol party, having much greater regard to the conditions under which they lived and the length of time they spent at sea. At the end of our detachment there was a surplus of beer/lager which was disposed of to our entire satisfaction.

The Squadron Direction Officer, Lieutenant Ian Colton was a prolific writer of aircrew songs mainly aimed at the fixed wing squadrons onboard. They were bawdy and politically totally incorrect although we had no idea what that meant in those days.

Little & Large. HMS Ark Royal and USS Nimitz alongside in Norfolk Naval Base, USA. 1976

Ministry of Defence Crown Copyright

824 Squadron flying flags for US Independence Day. Fort Lauderdale, Florida. 1976

Periscope view of an 824 Squadron Sea King HAS Mk 1. 1976

Ministry of Defence Crown Copyright 1976

A BBC film/recording crew arrived onboard to record the record 'Sailing' to follow up the TV series on Ark Royal. My copy of the record has myself, Tony Rogers and Nigel Hennel in a photograph on the back of the sleeve. We look fed up. We *were* fed up as we had been dragged up to the venue in the hangar and were sitting through rehearsals. On a brighter note we persuaded the producer to record our squadron song sheet and give us a master tape. In the bowels of ARK ROYAL the more junior aircrew slept in cabins with four or five bunks. The entire squadron crammed into one of these spaces, plus the producer plus one, and his equipment. We sang our hearts out and everyone must have lost a few pounds in the process. I still have the resultant tape 41 years later, locked away in my ditty box plus the 'hymn sheets'.

Into 1978, the pace of flying and exercises did not drop and in April the squadron embarked in HMS ARK ROYAL headed for Puerto Rico in the Caribbean. The exercise and range facilities off the US Naval Base at Roosevelt Roads at the eastern end of the island were extensive and with fewer restrictions compared to European ranges. Between late June and early August the squadron disembarked to NAS Jacksonville (Northern Florida) whilst HMS ARK ROYAL underwent a Maintenance Period in the nearby Naval Base at Mayport. A lot of squadron personnel took the opportunity to bring their families out from UK during this period and to take their Sumer Leave. As a part of continuation navigation training I organised to take two aircraft on two separate weekends to NAS New Orleans. NAS New Orleans is a vast airfield south of New Orleans which is home to the reserve air forces of the US Navy, Army and Air Force. In addition it has a Coastguard Unit which stores aircraft commandeered from drug smugglers and the like. Having commandeered the aircraft they are then used in the fight against smuggling. As the airfield is primarily used by the reserve forces it is very busy at weekends. Booking accommodation through the US Navy meant our accommodation in New Orleans was relatively cheap. Once the squadron aircraft had been secured for the weekend, the crew, maintainers and passengers were free to enjoy New Orleans until it was time to leave on the Monday morning. I do remember a breakfast of ice cream and Oysters in Jackson Square as the sun was coming up. Flying from NAS Jax to NAS New Orleans was enlivened by flying over the Suwannee River and singing the lyrics of 'Way Down the Swanee River'!

Then it was back across to the North Atlantic for the October exercise Display Determination and into the Mediterranean for some minor NATO exercises.

Perhaps one of the proudest moments on 824 Squadron was meeting the Queen Mother. ARK ROYAL was operating in the Moray Firth in September 1978. The Queen Mother was at Mey Castle in Caithness and having launched the ship in 1950 had asked to pay one last visit to the ship. The weather was marginal but apparently the Queen Mother was insistent, so the visit went ahead. Representatives from all departments were to meet Her Majesty on the Quarterdeck. At the appointed hour we squadron 'Wheels' were in their place. Our group was four; we were all introduced and the Queen Mother started to speak. She addressed us all at the same time, but I felt she was talking to me personally. Later we all agreed we felt the same. I cannot remember what was said apart from that she loved travelling by helicopter, it was just the manner in which it was carried out! It was an amazing experience. I spoke to her second lady-in-waiting, who I considered was too old to be visiting an aircraft carrier, but who told me she was the proud holder of Helicopter Pilot Licence No 1 which she had achieved in the 20s.

I left HMS ARK ROYAL and 824 Squadron in Majorca, flying out from Palma back to the UK to take up my next appointment in 706 Squadron.

Chapter 17

RNAS CULDROSE

706 Squadron/Sea King HAS 1.
January 1979 – January 1980

I was appointed the Senior Observer in 706 Squadron, the Operational Flying Training (OFT) unit responsible for the final training of Pilots, Observers and Aircrewmen before joining their Front Line squadrons. My primary responsibility was the period of training in RFA ENGADINE when the course was taken away to operate in a realistic operational scenario.

RFA ENGADINE was a helicopter support ship which could accommodate 3 Sea King (but only two in the hangar) and associated aircrew and maintainers. It had two operating spots. Part of the Operational Flying Training was a two to three week phase embarked in ENGADINE which culminated in an overnight stop somewhere in the UK, planned by the students, prior to returning to RNAS Culdrose.

In and around 1979 there were many discussions going on regarding having WRNS at sea and ENGADINE was seen as a useful trials vehicle. ENGADINE embarked a female Meteorology Officer which was fine until one of the students declared undying love for the lady in question. We also embarked a number of WRNS maintainers from 706 Squadron as it is easier to trial the integration of male and female maintainers on an RFA with civilian style accommodation than on a warship.

ENGADINE had what can only be described as a banana shape. Although designed as a helicopter support ship the flight deck was not level with the water line and there was a marked incline running from the stern down to the hangar. Extreme caution had to be exercised with aircraft moves, landings and take offs. The male maintainers were aware of this as most had sea experience already. But the result was that every WRNS maintainer appeared to have a shadow who was basically looking out for them. The situation was not helped by the fact that some of the WRNS had boyfriends back on the Squadron. The boyfriends ashore being more worried than their girlfriends onboard! I witnessed some tense moments during that detachment.

Two events which have nothing to do with flying come to mind. The first in late Summer when ENGADINE and the detachment were part of a major submarine exercise taking place in and around Gibraltar. There were a number of submarines taking part and Flag Officer Submarines decided that, once the exercise was over he would hold a cocktail party for his submariners alongside in Gibraltar and that ENGADINE would be the venue. The Master of ENGADINE and myself as Detachment Commander would be invited guests, but no one else. This effectively meant that the detachment had to fend for itself ashore for the evening.

A detachment 'committee of good taste' decided that the submariners should be held accountable for intruding into the aircraft world. My only stipulation was that the Master had to be aware of and agree with the committee's proposals and that none of our students were to be involved as they were at the beginning of their careers.

The basic plan was simple. The detachment instructors would provide four of the stewards responsible for dispensing the drinks and small eats, one of the submarine lifebelts which would greet guests at the gangway would mysteriously disappear to be held for ransom later, and once the Flag Officer and his retinue had left the remainder would be entertained by a Fleet Air Arm choir. The Master, who really would have preferred a quiet night onboard agreed the plan.

Royal Fleet Auxiliary Engadine. (1979)

Ministry of Defence Crown Copyright 1979

It was a beautiful evening, but I did not enjoy it! The sight of the four 'stewards' waltzing around the throng of guests with jugs of water topped up with tonic, or jugs of gin topped up with water, jugs brandy with no ginger or jugs of ginger with a little brandy, orange laced with vodka, and other variations I shudder to think about now. There was some magic ballet performed by one steward who managed to be in the act of offering a mini sausage roll whilst at the last moment turning away to talk to a guest who was complaining about his G&T. Another steward managed to chat up one of the female guests whilst spilling water down the sleeve of their male companion. It was difficult to appear to be normal whilst viewing all these antics going on around me. Goodness knows what I missed.

RFA Engadine with 706 Squadron Operational Flying Training Course Detachment overhead. 1979

Ministry of Defence Crown Copyright 1979

Once the Flag Officer had left and we were down to the more junior submarine officers the detachment 'choir' swung into action. The choir of three (all of whom had been 'stewarding' appeared on a raised platform at the back of the hangar. The leader, Lieutenant Rory McLean, had a party piece when by way of a very long sleeved jacket and false hands he managed to sing ' With these Hands' whilst extending the false hands. The submariners enjoyed it thinking it was part of the night's entertainment. The leader was now joined by his two songsters in their flying overalls and the three sang a selection of Fleet Air Arm songs, not all very complimentary to submariners (or anyone else for that matter). Despite all this, the trio were widely applauded although I did note a couple of submarine COs disappearing quickly down the gangway. We managed to purloin one of the submarine lifebelts which as far as I know it still exists as a 706 Squadron trophy at Culdrose. Vice Admiral Rory A.I. McLean CB, OBE sadly passed away in September 2021.

I mentioned already that the detachment would do a land-away the night before returning to Culdrose. One of these land-aways was to Colerne Barracks in deepest Wiltshire. Colerne had been an RAF base before being taken over by the Army.

The three aircraft landed by a former RAF hangar where we were met by an official car. Part of the exercise was to enable the students to take charge of securing the aircraft. As it had been a long hot sticky flight from ENGADINE I decided it was time to pull rank and take the transport to the Officers Mess and get a hot shower. No one around in the Officers Mess but there were keys out for our rooms. Took mine and wandered up the stairs to my room. Basic room, just a basin in the corner and I needed a shower.

Putting on my dressing gown I stepped out into the corridor expecting the ablutions to be somewhere on the same floor. Wrong! Down the long corridor came a very imposing blond female Army Major. When I say imposing I mean she was at least six inches taller than me and somewhat broader.

I politely asked her where the showers were and explained who I was. 'Come with me' was the response. Round a corner and then a U turn down some wide stairs. At this point she put her arm around my shoulder to guide me down the stairs – at that very moment the door opposite the bottom of the stairs opened and the detachment staff and students piled in. I am afraid the sight of me in my dressing gown being handled by an Army Major of imposing stature was just too much for them and the group just dissolved into laughter and amusement. I never did live that down.

This was my last official flying appointment as I departed for the Greenwich Staff Course and staff appointments for the rest of my naval career.

Chapter 18

FLASHING BLADES OVER THE SEA

1977-1979

In 1977 I decided that I had sufficient information and interest to write a small tome on the history of RN helicopters up to the present day. I had been spurred on by the Fleet Air Arm Museum looking for funds and a proportion of the profits from the book went to the Museum.

During my research I wrote to all helicopter squadrons asking for their histories, visited the Imperial War Museum, the Fleet Air Arm Museum, and made extensive use of the internet, such as it was in those days.

An 'oppo' from HMS BULWARK, Mike Critchley had left the RN and started up a book selling and publishing business - 'Maritime Books'. When Ian Allen rejected my book I turned to Mike and he agreed to publish. I needed a VIP to forward the book and one of our more illustrious Fleet Air Arm VIPs was the Prince of Wales. I approached him to write the forward. To my delight he agreed.

The book was published in Spring of 1980 with hardly 'rave' reviews, but they were not scathing.

Mike Critchley had 'fingers in all sorts of pies' and through his contacts he booked me onto BBC South West on their early evening programme South West Today, and onto the local radio early morning show. South West Today gave me an afternoon in the Plymouth TV studios and a chance to complain to their met forecaster Ian(?) Rich about their inaccurate forecasts. I have never seen the televised content of that interview as my set at home did not record. Those who watched it said it was OK. The early morning radio broadcast was a bit like being in a spy thriller. The local radio studio was in Truro. My instructions were to contact the receptionist in the hotel opposite the radio studio and ask for the studio key. Across the road armed with two keys, through two doors and into the recording studio, basically a small box with a microphone. At every stage there was a notice telling me what to do. There were various electrical switches to be made, in the right order, and eventually I was talking to someone in the Plymouth studio. A quick rehearsal and it was into the interview on air. Again I have no record of what was recorded, but those who were up early enough said it was fine. My TV and Radio career was over.

Flashing Blades over the Sea cover

Chapter 19

ROYAL NAVAL COLLEGE GREENWICH

No 58 RN Staff Course.
January - August 1980

An interesting phase of my naval life which broadened my horizons and forced me to apply myself to staff work.

Living in the college with all the history from days gone by and having meals and formal dinners in the Painted Hall was somewhat surreal. Access to the college library became useful to me as I was able to track my grandfathers' naval career through the extensive collection of Navy Lists (Yearly publication with details of all Naval Officers ranks, units, ships etc).

Somewhat like going back to school we studied English grammar, staff papers, the other two services, read a lot, and listened a lot. The weeks were busy and the weekend commute down to Cornwall on the Friday, returning on the Sunday evening was quite stressful.

We visited the Army at Paderborn Garrison in Germany, the RAF at RAF Scampton, and NATO Headquarters in Brussels.

Visits were highly organised and strictly 'shepherded' by the college staff. We, the students, felt we were being treated like sheep and whenever there was a mass movement to a coach or building cries of 'baa, baa' would be heard. Some wag, designed and ordered a No 58 Staff Course tie - blue, with the No 58 logo and a large white sheep emblazoned upon it. I still have mine.

At Paderborn we visited the Sennelager Training Area and toured various 'stands' from gun emplacements to tanks. The outstanding memory was the Mobile Bath Unit. Effectively a unit for decontaminating troops, the sheer enthusiasm and knowledge of those who were demonstrating the unit was amazing! At Scampton we saw Guy Gibson's dog's grave and witnessed a nuclear bomb loading onto an Avro Vulcan!

Nearer home we visited the Metropolitan Police Control Room where we were showed a video of a police helicopter monitoring a march across Westminster Bridge. The commentary included the lines 'just think, if I had a machine gun I could get rid of this lot'. Our host, apologising, said you should not have heard that!

A visit to the News of the World printing press in Fleet Street on a Saturday night was revealing. We started on the bottom floor where the type was set ready to print – that was hot and decidedly unpleasant. Then to the paper rolls weighing over a ton, each rotating ready to replace the roll which had just been finished – not a place in which to make a mistake. Then up again, to see the printed newspaper coming off the press and being made up into the familiar bundles by hand. One of our number asked why this process was not automated thereby doing away with the large numbers of people who appeared to be standing around. Luckily, in all the noise, none of the workers heard the question. Up to the next floor to offices with a bit of quiet. It was explained that since we had been in the building there had been sixteen industrial disputes of varying natures, all of which had been resolved. Our host said that if the comment about automation had been overheard they would have been into dispute number seventeen. Such were industrial relations in 1980.

There were many formal lectures during course, a large proportion from outside the college. Each outside lecturer would have a host nominated from our course. As luck would have it, I hosted the speaker from the Security Services. He was announced as a speaker from the Security Services – no name. At lunch, as the host, I sat with him. Try small talk with someone whose name you do not know, whose job is difficult to discuss, and whose private life needs to remain so!

One of our early speakers was David Owen, the Labour MP who had been Secretary of State for Foreign and Commonwealth Affairs from 1977 to 1979. Sitting towards the front of the lecture hall I was interested to note that as he started to speak his hands holding his notes were visibly shaking. David Owen's career relied on communication, and I found this shaking quite a revelation. I briefly spoke with David Owen afterwards and mentioned the shaking. He said he always had nerves before speaking to any group of people and it showed through his hands shaking.

Come the end of an enjoyable interlude in my career I learnt I had been appointed to the Directorate of Naval Air Warfare in the Ministry of Defence Main Building in London. Luckily through college contacts I was able to find accommodation in the Greenwich area for at least my first few months in the MOD.

Chapter 20

MINISTRY OF DEFENCE - DNAW/DOR(SEA)

29 October 1980 – September 1985

This period in my service life was probably the most varied and thought provoking. Living in Cornwall and working in London meant a lot of commuting sometimes by car, sometimes by train. For the first few months I lived in Greenwich, looking after a flat vacated by the barrister brother of Captain Peter Hoare who had gone to South Africa to work. I had inherited a bike from Lieutenant Commander Stan Turton who I relieved in the Current Helicopter Desk and the 7 mile daily commute to Main Building was either by train or bicycle dependent upon the weather. I never felt unsafe cycling around London and indeed the early morning cycle over Tower Bridge was a joy.

The Current Helicopter Desk had the responsibility of processing Naval Staff Requirements in regard to equipment used by back seat crews in all current RN helicopters through the Ministry of Defence procurement system. Plus in addition dealing with any other matter concerning back seat equipment or procedures that turned up – these were the most difficult!

Stan and I had a two week turnover. Every lunchtime we would set forth from Main Building to find a new CISCO restaurant. CISCO was the organisation which provided refreshment facilities for all civil service buildings in London. Stan's aim was to locate and eat lunch at every CISCO within a couple of miles of Main Building. Civil service buildings were identified by the dirty lace curtains which adorned those buildings. Using our Main Building passes we would enter and sniff our way to the CISCO facility.

We also did a handover! In an unguarded moment Stan said there were evenings when he made his way back to his 'hovel' in Tooting Bec and threw himself onto his bed crying his eyes out with frustration. After five years in the MOD I fully understood how he felt but I never got to the crying my eyes out stage. Working with my engineering counterpart in Director General Aircraft (Navy) (DGA(N)), I was responsible for all the back seat aspects of RN helicopters. A normal day started at about 0730 in the office which meant there was about an hour before the phones started ringing; the day ended at about 2030 which meant there was a good hour with no phones and 30 minutes' worth of sherry time and catching up with the day's news.

After a couple of years I moved from Greenwich into a room in Marsham Street which had been a maids room in by-gone days. I had access to a bath and toilet as well! As a resident in this room I was able to obtain a Westminster Council Car Parking Permit. There was a rigmarole to go through to get it and one night at 2130 there was a knock on the door of my room – it was a Westminster Council official checking up that I did indeed stay at this address. From Marsham Street it was a ten minute walk to the MOD past the Houses of Parliament or Westminster Cathedral, depending on how I felt.

Life in Main Building was never dull. I remember getting into the VIP lift by mistake at the same time as Michael Heseltine and his aide. I was about to offer the Minister a 'good morning ' but his aide looked daggers at me and shook his head. We stopped at the 4th floor for me whilst the lift continued to the 7th floor. I had to visit the Ministers office on the 7th floor on occasion. On one visit I was talking to the secretary when John Nott appeared in a bit of a rage, shouting and generally being obnoxious. I withdrew quickly.

I had a number of bosses during my time in MOD; Keith Hindle, Brian Skinner, Chris Quarrie, and one whose name I have forgotten! Keith moved his family up to London from Helston and bought a house in Brixton. He was very pleased with his purchase until the night he returned home, looked over the garden wall at the back and encountered the Brixton Riots.

On 2 April 1982 Argentina invaded the Falkland Islands and for the next ten weeks life in the Main Building changed. In peacetime Main Building was on the front line fighting for resources, i.e. men and equipment, to keep the armed forces viable. In wartime those front-line forces are doing the fighting backed up by Main Building assisting wherever possible.

The front seat Current Helicopter Desk Officer was Lt Cdr Colin Young. He, I, and Director General Aircraft (Navy) engineers very much worked together to support the front-line helicopter squadrons and flights.

In order to get equipment into service there was a set routine of papers, committees and the like, backed up with studies etc etc. We were now faced with a situation where we needed to obtain equipment quickly. Colin and I designed an Urgent Operational Requirement form (UOR) which contained all the relevant information needed to allow equipment under a certain financial ceiling to be authorised. Our Director, Captain Ben Bathurst liked it, we started using it and surprise, surprise, the Assistant Chiefs of Naval Staff began to sign it off, as did the Defence Secretariat (who held the purse strings). I believe a version of it is still in use today.

Life got very interesting and busy. Support to helicopter assets on their way south was top of my list. It became obvious that the spectre of real warfare had concentrated the minds of MOD suppliers and those responsible for monitoring and approving MOD spending. Procedures which would normally take weeks, even months, were now being actioned in days, sometimes hours. I was selected as the Naval Staff spokesman at the CCTV briefings given every morning to all staff in Main Building. This latter task involved obtaining a very high security clearance, higher even than the Prime Minister's clearance. During one of my briefings the CCTV system had a colour failure which caused the briefers face to turn green. I spent the rest of the day being asked if I had recovered from my illness!

On 4 May HMS Sheffeld was sunk by an Argentinian Exocet and the need for Airborne Early Warning (AEW) became crucial. The impetus behind providing a solution was immense. Since 1978 when the Gannet AEW3 had been decommissioned and AEW responsibility passed to the RAF there had been an unease about the lack of AEW cover for the Fleet. Many solutions were tentatively put forward by companies but finance and practicality had meant they were all rejected.

My boss, Commander Brian Skinner a 'junglie pilot', and I had a meeting with EMI who had approached us with a proposal to use a variant of the EMI Searchwater radar fitted in the Nimrod but fitted in a Sea King. From this meeting an UOR was raised for a feasibility study. The feasibility study was approved within hours! On 6 May a meeting of all interested parties was held in MOD driven by Captain Ben Bathurst, the Director of Naval Air Warfare. On 17 May the feasibility study reported its results. On 21 May a further UOR raised a requirement for the modification of four (later reduced to two) Sea King aircraft for AEW duties. A contract was signed on 25 May. In normal times this process would be estimated in years.

The project then continued to run at breakneck speed. Lt Cdr Peter Fluttcr, an ex 849 Gannet AEW3 observer had to assemble four ex AEW observers, four ASW Sea King observers and 2 Sea King pilots, and head up the resulting AEW Flight. Engineers of all trades had to be found, engineering decisions of all sort had to be made, flight clearances, trials programmes, the list was endless. My involvement was paperwork and supporting the various agencies in their engagement with the Ministry of Defence.

The first test flight occurred on 23 July and two AEW capable Sea Kings with aircrew and aircraft engineers joined HMS Illustrious on 2 August.

The gestation of the AEW Sea King has been well documented elsewhere. I believe the following, an extract from an article in James Navy International magazine sums up the AEW project perfectly;

On 4 May 1982, an AM-39 Exocet missile launched by a Super Etendard struck HMS Sheffield, one of the Type 42 radar pickets. It demonstrated the glaring gap in fleet air defence that had been opened up by the absence of maritime AEW.

To address this vulnerability, work was set in hand on 10 May to expedite the rapid development of an AEW capability for the fleet. This so-called LAST (Low Altitude Surveillance Task) effort drew on nascent concepts for an adaption of the Sea King anti-submarine helicopter equipped with an ARI 5980 Searchwater Mk 1 radar.

The gestation of LAST has become a stuff of legend. A feasibility study was completed on 17 May, and radar manufacturer Thorne-EMI received a contract to modify Searchwater for the AEW role eight days later. First equipment was delivered to Westland for installation in a Sea King within eight weeks of contract signature.

The conflict in the South Atlantic was over by the time the first two AEW-configured Sea Kings were delivered to the RN (they embarked aboard HMS ILLUSTRIOUS as D Flight of 824 Squadron on 2 August 1982). Nevertheless, the delivery of this contingency capability to the front line in the space of just 90 days remains a remarkable engineering achievement.

As the only Observer in the DNAW helicopter team I played my part in bringing the project to a successful conclusion. It was 90 days of full-on cooperation, goodwill and sheer hard work by a very motivated team of people.

I was awarded the MBE by Her Majesty the Queen on 14 October 1982.

DNAW plus the RAF Nimrod desk had an annual meeting with our French equivalents to discuss matters of mutual interest. The Paris meeting was enlivened by the UK team putting their watches back instead of forward and arriving late! We had lunch in a chateau outside Paris before catching our RAF aircraft back to the UK. Regrettably two of us had food poisoning from the mussels we ate on that Thursday lunchtime and I spent a weekend doubled up over the loo. Amazing what you remember!

In April 1983 I moved from the Current Helicopter Desk into the Future Helicopter Desk which primarily dealt with the EH101 or, as it was later to be called, the Merlin helicopter. In the meantime DNAW had become part of Directorate of Operational Requirements (Sea) or DOR(Sea).

The Merlin had originated in 1977 with a Naval Requirement to replace the Sea King. In 1981 the requirement became part of a joint project between the Royal Navy and the Italian Navy, Westland Helicopters and Augusta. Westland and Augusta formed a joint company, European Helicopter Industries (EHI) to progress the project. The EH101 was originally European Helicopter 01. Due to a typing error at some point in the bidding process it came to be known as EH101!

My involvement with the EH101 was the avionics and weapon fit. It was to carry four Stingray torpedoes or Mk 11 Depth Charges, and be fitted with a Blue Kestrel Radar with all round visibility, an integrated GPS and inertial navigation system, AQS 910 acoustic processor, carry mini-sonobuoys and a long range dipping sonar. It had three engines, and the pilot had lost the old fashioned dials to be replaced with digital screens. The aim was that night operation would be one pilot as opposed to two in the Sea King.

As the project progressed there were joint meetings in either London or Milan/Rome. Milan meetings were good as it involved an overnight stay in Stresa on Lake Maggiore before meeting in the Augusta factory. The Rome meetings were with the Italian

An operational Sea King ASaC Mk 7

Reproduced with the kind permission of Peter Mitrovitch

Sea King ASaC Mk 7 showing the 'bag' in stowed position.

Reproduced with the kind permission of Peter Webber

Augusta 'plastic' EH101 at Paris Air Show 1985

Navy and my everlasting memory is an evening meal in a Rome courtyard with all 37 delegates to the meeting. A waiter came round to each person and took their order without pen and paper; all orders appeared in the correct arrangement around the table. A real feat of memory!

At one early meeting in 1985 at the Augusta factory as the combined RN/Westland team arrived, we, the RN delegates were split off from the Westland attendees. Sworn to secrecy we were taken into a small hangar and shown a live sized plastic model of the EH101 under construction. It had been built by Augusta without telling Westlands. It was to be exhibited at the Paris Air Show later that year.

The EH101 first flew in 1987 by which time I had left the Future Helicopter desk. 35 years on I watch Merlin's flying overhead and I am proud that there is a little bit of me in them, however small that part may be.

The aviation section of DOR(Sea) were invited to the Orly Airshow in Paris. My memories from that visit are seeing a plastic

EH101 on display(!) and my one trip in an airship. Airship Industries only founded in 1980 were always keen to let the RN know their future plans and offered to us a trip in their Skyship 500. It was a very pleasant 30 minutes flight to the south of Orly. Airship Industries only lasted another couple of years and airships never really took off.

Another major part of my time in the Future Helicopter desk was in assisting UK companies selling the Sea King Mk 5 to the Indian Navy.

The Sea King HAS Mk 5 had developed from the Mk 1, through the Mk 2. The threat was changing, nuclear powered submarines were in the majority and the way to detect the threat lay in acoustic processors. This was achieved by lowering hydrophones into the water to listen to the underwater signature of a nuclear submarine which might be generated by pumps, main machinery, or propellors.

The Sea King HAS Mk 5 was upgraded with an MEL Sea Searcher radar, an AQS 902 acoustic processor plus a suite of mini-sonobuoys. As I had not served in a Mk 5 squadron I attended a Sonics Course in October 1980 at the Helicopter Analysis Unit (HAU) at RNAS Culdrose.

The Indian Fleet Air Arm already had Sea Kings. The Mk 5 had the passive acoustic equipment which the Indian Navy were very keen to obtain. Commander Chris Quarrie (my then boss) and I were part of a combined Westlands/ Marconi team which travelled out to New Delhi on a sales mission. We were put up in the UK High Commission in Delhi. There were many meetings and presentations. Readers may be familiar with pictures of the Government Buildings in Delhi designed by Edward Lutyens, in beautiful rows, in beautiful sandstone. The Indian Navy equivalent of DNAW was located to the rear of these buildings in what I can only describe as a mud hut. On our first visit we were offered tea in cracked cups which I guessed had never seen a washing up basin.

The Westland agent in New Delhi organised an official party for us at his residence. We arrived by car early in the evening just as it was getting dark. Getting out of the car we were surrounded by beggars and other street dwellers and were ushered swiftly into what appeared to be the worlds biggest marquee. The contrast from outside to inside remains with me. Inside there were carpets, bright lights, music and around the marquee were food and drink stalls. This was hospitality with no budget. Outside was abject poverty. The evening passed in somewhat of a haze.

There was a day off, so Chris and I decided to visit the Taj Mahal. The High Commission staff organised us to travel by train down to Agra, some 110 miles south. Unfortunately the day before we were due to go the train was cancelled and we had to take a bus which meant an early start for the 5 hour journey. This was the white knuckle ride to end all white knuckle rides. The road was a single carriageway with two way traffic. Vehicles dared each other to be the first to give way. However we reached Agra without incident! We managed to visit both the Taj Mahal and the Agra Red Fort and to have lunch in the Agra Hilton. Lunch was enlivened by the sight of a rat walking around the dining room on a dado rail around the wall. No-one seemed to think this was unusual and the rat ambled around in a leisurely fashion. Both of us slept for the entire journey back to New Delhi!

Some months later, with sales negotiations still proceeding the Indian Navy invited Marconi back to New Delhi for more talks. Marconi invited me to accompany the 'salesman' on this trip. No High Commission this time and we were accommodated in the Oberoi Hotel, a monstrosity of a concrete building. No parties, a lot of meetings and questions and the Indian Navy made its mind up very quickly. We were clear to return to the UK. All economy/ business class flights to the UK were booked over the next few days but the Marconi salesman managed to persuade the firm that unless we took the only flight available, a first class PANAM flight leaving that night, we would be stuck here until Christmas! We duly caught Flight PANAM 1 which flew from Houston, Texas, around the world, and back to Houston. So for the next few hours I lapped up first class hospitality in the nose of the Boeing 747. On arrival over Heathrow we were informed that a Nigerian aircraft had run off one of the runways and there would be a delay in landing. During this delay an elderly Indian lady came through the curtains into the first class compartment. After a few seconds she started to scream. Immediately a flight attendant was there beside her. She continued screaming until the flight attendant calmed her down and asked what was the problem. The passenger had expected to see pilots in the forward cabin but all she could see was where the nose came to a point and she had panicked thinking there were no pilots in control.

All good things have to come to an end. I slipped out of the Ministry of Defence for the last time, returned home, and prepared to face my next challenge – Operations Officer at RNAS Culdrose.

Augusta/Westland Merlin HM2

Reproduced with the kind permission of Nick Weight

Chapter 21

RNAS CULDROSE

Operations Officer.
September 1985 - December 1987

Back to Culdrose where for the first time I would become a member of the ships company rather than as part of a lodger unit on the Air Station.

RNAS Culdrose was commanded by a Captain RN, aviation specialist, supported by various Heads of Department (HODs). The Commander, normally not an aviation specialist but a straight seaman, was Second in Command and responsible for day to day activities such as discipline, ceremonial, security, morale etc. Commanders covering the Air, Medical, Supply, and Air Engineering Departments completed the naval Heads of Department. There was also a Civilian Administration Officer.

In turn, Commander(Air), Commander Simon Thornewill, had four officers reporting to him, the Senior Air Traffic Control Officer responsible for Air Traffic Control services on the airfield; the Meteorological Officer responsible for provision of weather services; Lieutenant Commander (Flying) responsible for aircraft movements within the airfield and Flight Safety; and the Operations Officer responsible for coordinating Culdrose air activities outside of the airfield boundary and Search & Rescue. Inevitably responsibilities overlapped and it was important that all worked together. This team facilitated the activities of the Culdrose Training and Front Line squadrons, the Flight Deck Training Unit, the Fire Services, Safety Equipment section etc.

As the Operations Officer I had a very satisfying job when everything was going well! My domain was in the Control Tower with an Assistant Operations Officer, a Chief Petty Officer WRNS as supervisor in the Operations Room and six WRNS as watchkeepers. I am sure the six WRNS were selected for their attractiveness and there was a steady flow of junior aircrew through the Ops Room asking the simplest of questions. There were at least two marriages as a result of these visits.

The Admiralty had purchased the land in 1944 with the aim of setting up a fixed wing airfield for ten years. Originally given the name HMS COUGH (RNAS Helston) after the Cornish bird. However, the Lords of the Admiralty changed this to HMS SEAHAWK (RNAS Culdrose) when it was commissioned in April 1947. Still going strong 73 years after commissioning it has been home to all Fleet Air Arm aircraft types over the years. I have been unable to unearth from where the name Culdrose originated. Through the 1980s it had the most airfield movements in UK and the Operations Room was kept busy.

Planning ahead and keeping operations on an even keel were important to me in this job and maybe that is why I have few recollections or stories of note from my time as 'Ops'. My task was aided by an Assistant Operations Officer. During my time I had three different assistants. To my sorrow I cannot remember the name of the first incumbent. He was a Chief Petty Officer with a long and distinguished career. For his leaving 'do' I organised a Heron from Station Flight at RNAS Yeovilton to take the Ops Team from Culdrose to Guernsey for lunch (navigational exercise!). He was very surprised to be told to turn up in civvies that morning. Second assistant was Warrant Officer Aircrewman Seed whose aviation knowledge and experience were invaluable to me. Third assistant was a brand new Special Duties Sub Lieutenant straight out of training having been promoted from the Lower Deck, John Francis. With little aviation background he launched himself into the job with enthusiasm and a real can-do attitude.

Their contribution to operations at Culdrose during my time there cannot be underestimated.

One event which could not have been predicted was in April 1986. As I drove into the airfield at about 0730 on a Monday morning I could not help noticing it was starting to snow. Parked up and made my way up to the Ops Room. There was a view to the airfield perimeter and the main road from Helston had what appeared to be some stationary traffic. Within minutes the snow fall increased and visibility to the perimeter was lost. The airfield closed, declared BLACK, and all eyes turned to the meteorology department who had failed to predict this weather. The snowstorm raged for the whole day covering all ground to the West of Culdrose but amazingly some ten miles to the East near Truro there was little to no snow. By late afternoon it was obvious no one was going home and preparations were made to accommodate all personnel on the base. The conditions were sub arctic and arrangements were made for Land Rovers to ferry people from their place of work to the accommodation blocks. A Land Rover arrived at the Control Tower and half a dozen of us piled in. Conditions were atrocious as we drove very slowly towards the main airfield road. We first encountered a large hangar door which was on the left of the slip road. Then a gentle stop as we came up against the low wall around the static water tank. Any faster and we may all have drowned! Eventually we were over the bridge and into the accommodation area but could only get within 150 yards of the Wardroom. So it was out and get to the Wardroom front door as fast as possible in the appalling conditions. The following day the snow showers had eased but there was still the snow that had fallen to be dealt with. The snow clearing equipment on the base was just not capable of dealing with the amount of snow that had fallen. By Wednesday morning things were getting back to normal but there were some enormous heaps of snow littered all over the airfield. I eventually arrived home on Wednesday evening looking forward to a bath and some clean clothes. The weathermen assured us this had been a freak occurrence which they could not have predicted, especially in April. In the accompanying photograph the Control

Tower, now replaced with a modern version, can be seen with the slip road leading away to the left. The hangar we first met is just off the photo but the round static water tank can plainly be seen.

In the summer of 1986 Culdrose was due an Admiral's Inspection when over two days every department would be examined from its paperwork through to its procedures and readiness for any eventuality including security. The Culdrose Command decided that there would be a rehearsal Inspection and I was given the task of organising the detail. There are many things that can be made to happen just by making a broadcast over the station tannoy and then checking that the correct actions had been taken.

But there was an emphasis on security at the time and airfields by their nature are attractive targets. I decided we needed some reality in the rehearsal and contacted the local Territorial Army unit.

I explained what I was looking for - basically a threat from persons unknown who were infiltrating the airfield. The rules were outlined, no trespassing on the main runway, no entering buildings, no violent resisting arrest, no damage etc. I was happy that Culdrose personnel would have a threat to counter albeit without the resistance they might encounter in a real situation, in addition to all the other evolutions that were required by my scenario. The Territorial Army were very happy to cooperate. This was out of the ordinary and they could make up their own plan of action.

The day started well enough, everything appeared to be running to my script. Mid-morning there were reports of persons to the east side of the airfield coming over the perimeter fence and within minutes they were sitting down on the main runway whilst others were heading for squadron buildings and using force to get inside. Then the Control Tower was seized and in the office above mine, Commander(Air), the head of the Air Department was being held at gunpoint. This was not in the rehearsal plan! Cdr(Air)

RNAS Culdrose aircraft formation. 1986

Ministry of Defence Crown Copyright 1986

called off the rest of the rehearsal and I spent the remainder of the day on the phone dis-organising events and apologising!

The OIC of the Territorial Army unit had decided to make it a realistic exercise with two aims, one to stop us operating aircraft and secondly to take out The Command. Both of which he did! We did pass our more formal Admiral's Inspection later on that summer, so Commander(Air) partially forgave me.

Meanwhile on the other side of the world in Hong Kong the HK Maritime Police were requesting a permanent Royal Navy Liaison Officer (RNLO) be present in their Operations Room in order to coordinate Maritime Police, Royal Navy and Royal Marine operations against Illegal Immigrants (IIs) attempting to get into Hong Kong by sea. The RN staff in HMS TAMAR could not provide an RNLO so a call went out throughout the RN for qualified officers to be spared for six weeks at a time to fill the RNLO post. I brought this to Cdr(Air)'s attention and he agreed that both my Assistant Operations Officer, Sub Lieutenant John Francis and myself could be spared, but not at the same time! We applied and were both accepted.

I was able to take my wife, Fiona, and son John to Hong Kong via an Indulgence flight on an RAF trooping flight and the Army provided a Married Quarter. I started my watchkeeping on 16 Jun 87. As a familiarisation to the task all watchkeepers had to complete a night patrol with the Royal Marines and a day on an RN Patrol Vessel. The patrol with the RMs was an experience.

RNAS Culdrose Control Tower 1986. Note the circular static water tank on far left of photo by the car park.

Ministry of Defence Crown Copyright 1986

From HMS TAMAR we set out in three Rigid Inflatable Boats (RIBs). A Corporal and myself in one, and two RMs in each of the other two.

It was just getting dark as we sped westwards through Hong Kong harbour. In a manoeuvre designed to 'scare' new crew members the three RIBs sped directly, but at an angle, at what appeared to be a solid wooden jetty. At the last moment it became obvious the solid jetty was an optical illusion and was made up of vertical piles equally spaced out through which the three RIBs passed with inches to spare. The Corporal smiled.

Navigation lights were extinguished and we slid into Mirs Bay where illegal immigrants were known to come across in boats at night. Keeping station without navigation lights in a RIB is only possible by closely following the wake of the RIB in front. The Corporal said 'you have control' and all of a sudden I did! The rest of the night was taken up with high speed movement followed by 30 minutes of dead silence. Needless to say we did not detect anything and returned to HMS TAMAR at daybreak. An interesting experience. The trip on the Patrol Vessel HMS STARLING was routine and not that interesting.

Life in the Maritime Police Operation Room was routine. There were other diversions. Our Army Married Quarter was just below Lion Rock, almost the highest place overlooking Kowloon and in the distance Hong Kong Island. We could watch aircraft flying into Kai Tak from our balcony and the views were to die for. We could go shopping around Hong Kong Island (Stanley was a favourite) and Kowloon (Nathan Road), and an evening stroll around Temple Street market was always enjoyable.

We organised a trip into China. It was a round trip starting with a hydrofoil ride to Shenzen. On arrival at the hydrofoil berth our passports were examined which led to me being taken to one side. My passport did not have an entry into Hong Kong stamp in it. This stamp was not required for UK military personnel. After a heart stopping few minutes I was allowed to board. A fast trip to Shenzen where we first visited a school and sitting on tiny chairs we were entertained by the children singing and dancing. Next to the Xian Warrior exhibition where there were half a dozen of the warriors brought down from Xian. All back on the coach and we drove up country, stopping to see the water buffalo pulling the ploughs in the rice fields which lined the road. We arrived in Dongguan at an hotel for lunch. The very enjoyable lunch was typical Chinese food with chopsticks. After lunch we thought to go for a walk outside of the hotel. No chance, as armed guards just outside the hotel perimeter made clear that we could not leave.

Back in the bus and onto Guangzhou (formerly Canton). We visited the Six Banyan Pagoda built originally in the 6th century and the Sun Yat-sen Memorial Hall. Next the zoo to see the pandas. Unfortunately they were not the black and white pandas that we had expected, but, the Red Panda.

Back on the bus and it was now rush hour. Bicycles were everywhere, you could not move for bicycles. The courier said this happens three times a day at shift changes and is not a good time for other vehicles. Into the station for our train back to Hong Kong. We were parched as it had been a hot tiring day. We tried to buy a Coke and found we did not have enough money. At last our train arrived and we gratefully found our seats in air-conditioned comfort. The seats were very comfortable and we slowly made our way to Hong Kong with a constant stream of souvenir sellers passing through the coaches. I was expecting the same problem with my passport as we passed into Hong Kong, but no, not a problem. We took the MTR tube to Lion Rock followed by the mini-bus virtually up to our door. We found public transport in Hong Kong was superb, friendly, cheap and safe.

Fiona had a distant cousin in Hong Kong who was serving with the Hong Kong Police. We got in touch and were invited to dinner in their apartment overlooking the Happy Valley race-course. He was involved in counter-terrorism and his Chinese wife was in Special Branch. As the time for the handover to China grew nearer, they were very aware that by the nature of their jobs and knowledge held they would have to relocate back to the UK.

Finally it was 24 July and the time came to leave. On an indulgence flight there is no guarantee of a seat as a serving military person can take your seat. It was an anxious wait to see if either Fiona or John had been removed from the flight. We were OK and enjoyed the 14 hour non-stop flight back to the UK.

Before I left for Hong Kong, Cdr(Air) had informed me that I was being put forward as the next Operations Officer on HMS ILLUSTRIOUS. This would be my penultimate appointment in the RN and I was looking forward to taking up the position. On our return from Hong Kong I was informed that the Captain of ILLUSTRIOUS, had refused to accept me as I was a Supplementary List officer and he wanted a General List officer in the appointment. A Supplementary List officer was both short-term and employed in a specific role, in my case aviation. A General List officer is a career officer with many options for specialising. I was therefore being appointed to the Joint Maritime Tactical School at RAF Turnhouse as Operations Officer(RN). At the time I was disappointed and probably upset, not least because I had been judged not capable of carrying out the role of a carrier Operations Officer. In hindsight I now see that this took us back to Scotland, led to my last naval appointment with Flag Officer Scotland and Northern Ireland which gave me the opening to become Naval Resettlement Information Officer for Scotland and Northern Ireland for 19 years. Had I gone to HMS ILLUSTRIOUS in all probability my last appointment would have been on the South Coast somewhere and the chance of setting in Scotland post retirement would have been very slim. Funny how things turn out for the best.

Chapter 22

RAF TURNHOUSE

Joint Maritime Operational Tactical School. (JMOTS)
RN Operations Officer.
January 1988 - February 1990

We moved into Army Married Quarters at Redford Barracks in Edinburgh as there were no naval quarters in Edinburgh. We later bought a house in the Buckstone area of Edinburgh.

JMOTS ran three courses a year with ships, submarines and aircraft from all NATO nations and some foreign navies participating. It was unique in that it gave all participants a week of work up exercises, with opportunities for live firing, followed by a week of a realistic tactical scenario. A de-briefing session with lessons learnt would then be held with all participants on the Monday following the two week exercise.

As the JMOTS RN Operations Officer my task was to coordinate the inputs from the air, the surface and sub-surface desks into a Work Up exercise plan and tactical scenario. I was also responsible for the debrief of all helicopter actions during the tactical phase. It was a busy appointment. From the moment of completing the debrief session from one course it was straight into planning for the next.

The Operation Order for each course ran to many pages and not all units received every part or section of the Op Order. All work stopped on the day that the Op Orders were collated. Every staff officer was involved in collecting the right pages on a trudge around tables full of paper piles.

The course was run from the Maritime Headquarters (MHQ) at Pitreavie. For two weeks we were watchkeeping in the subterranean Operations Room (known to all as The Hole). A considerable number of RN and RAF watchkeepers were required to keep events on track. An additional part of my duties was running the daily Helicopter Delivery Service (HDS) out to the ships off the north coast of Scotland. There was a constant stream of personnel and stores going to and from the task force and the HDS was provided by Bristow Helicopters at Aberdeen.

All units returned to their ports or other destinations on the Friday and records arrived at RAF Turnhouse to be analysed over the weekend ready for the debrief on the Monday. On JMCs with a large number of participants who would be scattered over many ports and airfields in Scotland, and beyond, this was a logistical nightmare.

Each course had a nominated Office in Tactical Command (OTC). Normally a UK Flag Officer but from time to time the Netherlands provided the OTC. JMOTS Staff would give the designated OTC a brief on the form of the course and some hints to help them during the course. This was information which we stressed should be retained by those being briefed and not disseminated. On one occasion we briefed the Netherlands Flag Officer in his base at Den Helder and unfortunately it became obvious once the course began that the information had been passed on to all the Dutch participants.

During a briefing to Flag Officer 1st Flotilla (FOF1) and his staff we were concealing the fact that a German Task Force proceeding across the Atlantic back to its base in Germany had agreed to become an unscheduled part of the tactical phase. Within JMOTS it had been agreed that the planned 'real' encounter would not be divulged to FOF1. However during the briefing it became obvious that FOF1 staff were aware that the German Task Force was in transit during the course. The question was asked, is the German Task Force going to be involved in the course? As I was the overall planner the JMOTS team turned to me for the response, No, was my response, the first time I had deliberately lied to an Admiral.

A busy and rewarding time for me but the RN wanted to move me on. Looking towards my final appointment in the Royal Navy it was a logical move to join the staff of Flag Officer Scotland and Northern Ireland based in MHQ Pitreavie. I was familiar with the MHQ and its staff and the area for which the Flag Officer was responsible. Domestically Fiona and I remained in our Edinburgh home.

Chapter 23

FLAG OFFICER SCOTLAND AND NORTHERN IRELAND

MHQ Pitreavie. Assistant Staff Plans Officer – March 1990 to February 1992

As the Assistant Staff Plans Officer (ASPO) I was part of a team of three officers responsible for National Exercise and War Planning for Flag Officer Scotland and Northern Ireland (FOSNI). In his NATO 'hat' FOSNI was COMNORLANT, Commander Northern Atlantic, and our national plans had to dovetail into NATO War Plans as well.

I had the pleasure of visiting RN and Army units in out of way places in Scotland in my two years. Whilst visiting the Loch Ewe Oil Fuel Depot I was sitting in the Drumchork Hotel overlooking Aultbea watching an enormous storm, which devasted most of the trees in Wester Ross raging outside, and wondering if the hotel would survive. That remains with me.

A NATO conference in Lisbon on the forthcoming WINTEX exercise was interesting for all the wrong reasons. The RN staff officer on COMIBERLANTs staff in Lisbon organised for all the delegates to have a tour of Lisbon on the tram system followed by a dinner in a Port Lodge. After a day's work delegates filed into two Lisbon trams complete with bars! The trams followed a route through Lisbon which can only be described as exciting. Through narrow streets which looked impossible to pass through, up hills and down dales, and all the while the bars remained open. The journey ended at the Port Lodge with a splendid meal and lots of Port. We all agreed this was NATO solidarity at its best!

Pitreavie Castle had an interesting history. Bought in 1938 by the RAF as a Coastal Command Headquarters it changed to a joint RAF/RN Combined Headquarters in 1939. A subterranean operations room was built. Towards the end of WW2 wooden huts were relocated from RAF Donibristle nearby in Fife. The huts had been at Donibristle since WW1. As a Duty Staff Officer I was required to stay onboard and live in Pitreavie Castle which doubled as the Wardroom Mess for the joint RN/RAF Staff at the MHQ. As Duty Staff Officer you were allocated a room in one of the huts as sleeping accommodation. There had been little maintenance since WW2 (or maybe WW1!) and every time the wind blew the whole hut would shudder. There was also a rumour about a ghost said to have haunted the castle and grounds, but I saw nothing! Pitreavie was the designated 'alternate' MHQ to take over defence responsibilities in the event that the national Northwood Headquarters were incapacitated. The 1994 Defence Review saw no use for MHQ Pitreavie, and it finally closed on 31 January 1996.

In my COMNORLANT Staff Officer 'hat' I was required to do the NATO Nuclear Weapon Release Procedure Course at Oberammergau in Germany. Somehow I obtained permission to drive to Oberammergau, it was always more difficult with NATO travel. Rumour had it that the American PX in Garmish Parten Kirken which served a US Army Barracks was worth a visit to get petrol coupons and Fisher Price toys! The petrol coupons would enable me to get a discount off fuel across Europe. I knew I would need US Dollars to buy anything in the PX.

During the first week of the course one afternoon was given up to cultural activities, like visiting the village of Oberammergau. I sped into Garmish Parten Kircken to visit the PX.

First task to get the petrol coupons. Into a small office with a clerk behind a wire mesh. I gave him my details and a 20 dollar note in payment. After looking at the details he asked me to take a seat, and disappeared. I sat there for about ten minutes and then realised there was someone looking at me over my shoulder, a US military policeman (a Bluebell). Two Bluebells then arrived in front of me, plus a person in civilian clothes, and I was asked to 'come with me'. At this point I had no idea what was happening, but you do not argue with two armed Bluebells.

We marched across a parade ground, into a very grand building, and finally into an office which was the largest I had ever seen with an enormously high ceiling and in the centre a small desk. The civilian invited me to take a seat in front of the desk. He identified himself as Bill Cottrell, Special Agent, looking into counterfeit dollars, and informed me I had just passed a counterfeit 20 US dollar note to the clerk in the PX. He told me I was under arrest.

By way of elucidation I explained that before leaving Edinburgh I had obtained four 20 US dollar notes from AT Mays, a national chain of travel agents. He took down all the details, and contacted his office in Paris, with details of the four notes. How long we sat there in silence I cannot remember, but eventually the phone rang out, the upshot of which was that my story checked out. The travel agent had been contacted and confirmed my story. The Special Agent then informed me I had been de-arrested. He gave me a form confirming receipt of my dollar bills. I returned to the car, drove out of the barracks and phoned home. I was quite shaken up by the experience. Never did get the petrol coupons, the Fisher Price toys, or even my dollars back. Later on that year I read an article about the flood of counterfeit US dollars in Europe and the strenuous efforts to find out where they were coming from. I learnt that the notes I had bought in Edinburgh were bought from a traveller at the AT Mays office in Newcastle.

I was a team member of the Flag Officer Scotland and Northern Ireland Offshore Emergency Response Group which was in place to provide the Command and Control of a security situation offshore. Procedures were, and probably still are, to coordinate action by UK & Norwegian Armed Forces, UK & Norwegian

Police and Offshore Companies. Likely scenarios involved attacks on oil rigs in the North and Norwegian Seas. Leading up to a joint exercise run from Norway a Chief Superintendent from the Grampian Police and myself attended a joint planning meeting in Oslo.

The 'Super' and I were put up in a very grand hotel in Oslo, the Continental Hotel. Maybe the Norwegians were paying! Anyway, after a gruelling day of meetings and planning, the 'Super' and I were enjoying a quiet beer in the hotel bar. Close behind our bar stools was a wall and there was a door to my right. All of a sudden I was forcibly pushed from behind, to be followed by a second push as the second person made their way from the door to a reserved area about twenty feet away. The first push was delivered by a very large rotund person in a black suit with an earpiece and microphone, the second push had been delivered by Frank Sinatra.

The reserved area was now full of Frank Sinatra and a number of large men in black suits, earpieces and microphones. Frank Sinatra was appearing in Oslo and was staying in the hotel. Here was a chance to get Frank Sinatra's autograph. I approached one of his security men, as wide as he was tall, and asked if there any chance of his autograph. Yes, later, he said. The Super and I sat and watched the goings on. All Frank Sinatra had to do was to raise a hand or an eyebrow and someone was at his side to take an order. We spoke with the bar-tender who told us that the resident pianist had been asked to play some Frank Sinatra tunes. Earlier during Frank Sinatra's stay another pianist had not come up to Frank's standard and had been ordered out of the hotel! You could feel the tension in the bar but the pianist passed muster, Frank Sinatra smiled and the men in suits visibly relaxed.

Just after midnight the men in suits had a shift change and I thought it a good time to ask again about an autograph. This time the response was 'not a chance'. Having had a busy day and up for an early flight back to Aberdeen the next morning the 'Super' and I retired to our rooms. An interesting encounter.

I was due to retire on 2 April 1992 after 32 years in the service. I went through the resettlement system and in doing so learnt that the post of Naval Resettlement Officer Scotland and Northern Ireland (NRIO Scotland), a Retired Officer Grade 2 was becoming vacant in February. Based in HMS COCHRANE, Rosyth, the NRIO had the remit of facilitating RN personnel into civilian employment. I applied for the post. Much to my surprise I was successful at interview and was asked to take up the post early. My resettlement plan had included an HGV driving course which I now forfeited. The RN released me in February 1992 and I found myself travelling from Edinburgh to HMS COCHRANE instead of MHQ Pitreavie wearing a suit instead of a uniform.

However, I had first to receive my last 'flimsy', which said,

MILNE has been a most effective and dedicated staff, utterly reliable, hardworking and meticulous, and he has readily taken on extra work as the situation dictates. His quiet and unassuming manner conceals a sharp intellect and a precise enquiring mind. Thoroughly professional in all he undertakes he has done particularly well as an important member of the Staff Command planning team in adapting to the changed circumstances of the Defence scene today. It has been a great pleasure to serve with him and I shall miss his logical and unwavering support. The Royal Navy will be the poorer without him on the Active List.

Signed Vice Admiral Hugo White.

I left with my head held high. A new world beckoned.

ABOUT THE AUTHOR

James Milne was born in Salisbury, Wiltshire in 1942.

Following education at Abingdon School, Abingdon, Berkshire, he joined the Royal Navy in 1960, selected for Observer training.

Retiring in 1992 he took up the post of Naval Resettlement Officer for Scotland and Northern Ireland as a Retired Officer 2 until 2011. He lives in Garelochhead close to the Clyde with his wife Fiona and will celebrate 60 years of marriage in 2022. He is the author of 'Flashing Blades over the Sea' concerning the development and history of helicopters in the Royal Navy. He was awarded the MBE in 1982.

In 2011 he joined the Board of Management of Argyll Community Housing Association, the 8th largest in Scotland. He was Chair of the Board from 2015 to 2020 and remains a Board member committed to the provision of first class social housing across Argyll and Bute.

JMM   18 Sep 21

Lightning Source UK Ltd.
Milton Keynes UK
UKHW020653261121
394628UK00006B/151

9 781839 758119